BLAME IT ON YOUR PAST LIVES

BLAME IT ON YOUR PAST LIVES

Personal Problems & Supernatural Solutions

TARA SUTPHEN

From Valley of the Sun

350+ audio/video tape titles:
Self-Help, Self-Exploration & Audio Books.
Master of Life Winners is a quarterly magazine mailed free.
Write for a copy.

First Edition: January 1993

Valley of the Sun Publishing, Box 38, Malibu, CA 90265

ISBN Number 0-87554-526-2
Library of Congress Card Number 92-090865

Dedication

To my husband Richard
May the glow of our love span the realm of time

Special Acknowledgements

Jason McKean for being a great brother and talented artist, Sharon Boyd for all the editing of this book and her encouragement, and Jess Stearn for being a dear friend and leading me to my destiny.

An "I love you" to Richard, William, Hunter, Cheyenne, Travis, Jessi, Steven, Todd, Scott, Sheila, and Sage; and my father Richard; my mother Marianne; Ed, Tim, Scott, Jason and Amy.

Contents

In The Beginning

Many people who write to me or participate in my seminar sessions claim that their past lives are responsible for their current difficulties. I try to show them that while their suffering does relate to prior incarnations, until they recognize the futility of blame, they won't be able to free themselves from the effect.

When my children come to me, crying that he or she did such and such to so and so, I say, "The Sutphens don't believe in blame. What did you do to cause it? What can you learn from it?"

Blame is a direct contradiction of the Master of Life principles my husband Richard and I have been teaching for years. If karma is the basis of reality, you and you alone are responsible for your earthly circumstances, relationships, and the resulting experiences.

If this is so, why be so masochistic? Why did you marry Ralph, who turned out to be a Cro-Magnon throwback? Why put yourself in a financial bind the personal equivalent of the national debt? Why choose to be a black sheep in a blue family? Answer: for the opportunity to learn to rise above fear-based emotions and to pay off old karmic debts.

"It's easier to blame someone or something else," you say.

You're right, it's easier. But it's a lot like swimming against the tide—you don't make any progress.

I contend that you are here on earth to **make progress**—to accomplish self-established goals. And if you can get in touch with the cause of your problems, you've taken the first step to resolving the effects. Then, if you're willing to be responsible for what you've created, you can act to change what is—evolving from the disharmony of blame into the harmony of living the life you want to live.

Obviously, not all problems relate back to past lives. Day-to-day choices can result in painful learning opportunities. But the source of an immature choice can often be found in unlearned lessons from past lives. Again, to understand today, you must look to yesterday. So that's where I'll begin.

When I began writing a "Cause and Effect" column using automatic writing in the Fall 1991 Issue of *Master of Life WINNERS*, neither Richard nor I were prepared for the immediate, total and overwhelming response of our readers. Because Richard's mail usually consists of letters asking philosophical and technical questions and challenges, which he addresses in his columns, *Controversial Questions and Answers*, and other articles and columns dealing with metaphysics and philosophy, many of our readers have turned to me with their questions concerning the basic interactions of life, such as love relationships, health, children, family, future career moves, et cetera.

I have always been intensely interested in people—what restricts them, what motivates them, and who they really are behind the masks society demands they wear—which is why I have devoted the last ten years to the study of handwriting analysis, palm reading, personology, and astrology. One day, while attempting to answer a letter, a little voice in my head kept saying, "Use your own ability to find the cause of their pain."

I decided to use automatic writing. It worked, and the response seemed appropriate although I did not know the letter writer.

Through the years, I have developed a wonderful relationship with my spirit guide Abenda, who has become both mentor and friend to me. She was very protective when I began automatic writing. In fact, for eight years, she only allowed me to have contact with herself, Richard's guides and the family's guides.

When I began to use automatic writing to answer questions in my column, Abenda set up rules about how I would conduct the automatic writing "interviews" with those on the other side. She didn't want any negativity in my temple room (the quiet, spiritual inner sanctum where I make contact with my guide), so we created a special contact room for these meetings. The experience of creating this environment required about three hours in deep trance. When we were finished, I had a comfortable, cozy spot to question the concerns of others and receive responses from their spirit guides, departed loved ones, or someone who knew them in a past life. Each session is always monitored by my own guide Abenda.

Although I have had years of verification of the automatic writing I've done for my own family, there is no way to know if you're on target when doing automatic writing for a stranger. Like any psychic technique, automatic writing isn't a science. But if past verifications are any indication of accuracy, in all probability, the information is valid. In the first few columns I did, I guess my insecurity was showing, because many whose questions I dealt with wrote to me again to thank me and to verify the information I had received.

Metaphysical author Jess Stearn, a dear family friend, relates a conversation he once had with Arthur Ford, the great medium. Ford had questioned the communications he received from his guide Fletcher, wondering if it was merely the dramatization of his own subconscious mind. Stearn responded to his doubts by saying, "Arthur, it really doesn't make much difference, does it? You don't know where the information is coming from, you haven't misrepresented anything. Maybe the information is coming from an experience you had before, or from a past life or from the Universal Intelligence. What difference does a name make? The only thing that really matters is the truth of whatever it is that came through you."

While I was working on this book, my Samoyed dog Tallinn ran away. I couldn't help but be concerned about her, though I tried to concentrate on the questions in the letters I had received. Several days later, in the middle of one session, Abenda gently set my mind at rest about my dog:

"Tallinn is just outside of Malibu. She is fine, but she does miss her family and home. Do put an ad in *Surfside News* [the local Malibu newspaper] and offer a small reward. But know that they want to keep her, though if she gets out, she'll try to come home. The day she got out of the yard her tag was on, but when someone grabbed her collar, she resisted and the collar came off. So, the person who found her doesn't have your address or phone information. Well, it's onward to do the work. You know that all works out for a reason. Remember that lesson. It's sometimes painful, but what is, is. —Love, Abenda"

I called the *Surfside News* and discovered that a woman had just called to place a found ad for my dog. The editor told me the woman had only wanted to say "Found: white dog," as she had become very attached to Tallinn and didn't want to give any particulars. I called to make arrangements to pick up my dog and noted her address—she lived just outside Malibu on county property.

When I arrived at her front door, the woman had tears in her eyes and confessed to me that she thought long and hard before placing the ad in the paper. "I really fell in love with her and wanted to keep her, but I knew whoever owned her would be heartbroken to lose such a beautiful dog." The woman had obviously lavished care and attention on Tallinn. White dogs are hard to keep clean, but Tallinn was freshly groomed, her fur snowy white, so I gave the woman a small reward and thanked her profusely.

Heading home on Pacific Coast Highway, Tallinn seated in the passenger seat, I had to laugh. Abenda knew that when the newspaper came off the press, I'd read the classified lost-and-found section, but she likes to prove her existence with little surprises.

From the missing dog episode, and many others too numerous to mention, I've learned that our guides are as capable of offering practical advice to assist us with the smallest aspects of life, as they are in answering the soul-searching existential questions we all ponder in the middle of the night.

One day, as I went to my temple room, considering what questions to ask, Abenda introduced me to a hearty, robust figure in a kilt who called himself the Duke of Invergordon. "But you may call me Rod," he said charmingly.

I decided to ask about the meaning of life and death. Abenda and I had discussed these things many times, but I was curious to see what this Scotsman had to say.

Rod Invergordon patiently waited for me to completely relax, then responded: "Many wonder, 'Why am I here? When will I die? What is my purpose?' Of course, the purpose is to gain a higher vibration and give love and compassion without reserve. To do this, think of the one source, and unite in and with the source. The great energy is what is known as God, but God is within all. At the moment of death, many people are scared, but there is no need to be. Fear is a silly emotion, very light and full of holes. You must know that without fear, you would be in Utopia, at the high level of the Godhead.

That is why it is necessary to deal with fear.

"Life is like a painting. How would you paint your portrait? What colors and surrounding things would be there? Is life to you an abstract conception or do you see the reality? Life is what you make of it, in some ways, and then comes karma—cause and effect—a multi-life balancing system that assures our soul growth. You can almost always carry out whatever karmic plan you established; you create this plan before you are born, with the help of an inter-life council. Sometimes you are pressured by the council to clean up matters that you would rather avoid.

"Disease is the carryover of all negative karma stored in its own energy vibration. Certain pollution, weather conditions, and polar exchanges let these disease molecules into the atmosphere. If you have a karmic configuration of chemical imbalance, you can trap the germ or energy within your own tissue, where it mutates to whatever form you carry with you. Cancers are caused by many elements that manifest a vibration, which invades the tissue just as bacteria does. You always experience disease for karmic reasons. You also have the power to probe your past to perceive the reasons.

"Why did you come here? The earth plane is where you learn of joy, pain, and fear. Love is joy, sorrow is pain, loneliness is fear. How can you be alone with so many entities surrounding you? Only you can surround yourself with barriers. Barriers to love, that create pain and fear. And these barriers exist within so many earth persons.You must mentally take down the barriers and open yourself to experience others and life. You can attract people who want to step into your light and aura, by opening to them, which is the first step to joy. Karmically, you attract others of a similar vibration, but you do not have karma with everyone you have contact with.

"Do you feel good about being on the earth? Do you not feel as though you've been given a great gift? Well, you have. We will continue on with these discussions. I enjoy coming to speak and write through you."

* * * * *

As individuals, one of our primary purposes is to search for our own truth, and having found it, to share it with the rest of humanity. In this book of questions and channeled answers, I hope to share some of my truth with you as you search for your own answers.

—Tara Sutphen
Malibu, CA, January 1993

Chapter One

Love Relationships

There is an old proverb that says "love makes the world go 'round." As we enter the New Age, more and more people are accepting that they were created whole and perfect beings whose purpose is to learn to give and receive unconditional love. This means to rise above judgment, blame and prejudice, and to accept others without expectations.

In this chapter, you will read many letters about relationship karma and the automatic writing I received in response. The importance of rising above resistance is a common thread running through these pages. We need to let go of our negative emotions and develop enough self-worth and self-esteem to assert our personal rights. It is a true expression of love to turn a negative situation into a positive challenge.

Relationships are one of the tools we use to work out our karma here on the earth plane. There are three kinds of relationships that help us do this: 1) family relation-

ships, which includes your immediate family and relatives; 2) love relationships, which includes soulmates,
lovers and mates, and 3) social relationships, which are
our friends, the community and even our enemies. Cas-
ual relationships usually are not karmic.

It takes effort to rise above negative karma. If a man
dates his secretary and his wife finds out, it's tempting to
get even instead of weighing the consequences. Are you
a person who thinks of consequences? Do you think
ahead to a good ending, a neutral ending, or a bad
ending? Or do you daydream five good endings and five
bad endings? How are you handling your karma in
relationships? Are you giving unconditional love or are
you finding excuses to create poor relationships?

I am always amazed at how people fool themselves
about what they really want in a relationship. I have a
couple of friends who say they want a good love relationship, then proceed to do everything in their power
to sabotage any possibility of love with someone who is
interested in them. Relationships aren't always easy; you
have to work at them. People look for a perfect dream
lover and ignore the real person knocking on their door.

Although harder for some than others due to karmic
background, we all have the ability to open our hearts
and allow love to resonate in our soul. Send love and
light to all who cross your path, and when you find love
that is reciprocated, you are blessed.

I have asked Abenda and Rod Invergordon to share
a little of their wisdom about love relationships with us.

Abenda wrote: "Love is such a beautiful state.
You are happy, you experience the oneness, and the

reason for living. You want to expand your horizons and give all you have to give. You trust in the process of life and know that life is worth living. Everyone has the potential to establish love relationships. Your individual karma predestines the duration of your euphoria. Many do not maintain a particular love for a lifetime. But any love between two people is a wonderful gift."

Rod Invergordon wrote: "Love relationships are one of the primary sources of pleasure and growth among your society. You come together again and again with people who love and cherish your soul. Initial recognition is usually very strong, often generating a feeling of ecstasy. Love relationships that dissolve usually do so because one partner's vibration is higher than the other's. Each person then goes on to follow their own karmic destiny. If there is unfinished business between the two people, it guarantees another meeting in another lifetime. In relationships, you must also be very careful what you ask for, because you often get exactly what you want and can end up where you didn't want to be.

"Soulmates are your very best friends who come again to reward your life. Usually, it was planned at the inter-life council. You may have difficulties, but they are usually very few and not with each other. Although there may be times of insecurities when the person leaves your life, the longing you feel usually brings your energies together in a future life. Tara, you have this bond with Richard and the children, though for different reasons with the children. But they are a reward in your life, and though everyday life may not always be easy, it is a grand existence."

Self-Destructive Soulmate

Q Dear Tara: My question is about my first husband, Eric. We met at work in 1986. The very first time we glanced at each other, we both knew that we were destined to be together. We fell in love and were married three months later. I thought I had found my soulmate, we were so spiritually connected. He was my knight in shining armor. After we married, we quit our jobs and moved to the West Coast. Within four months, our lives began to unravel as he began to indulge in drugs to excess. I had to leave; I am a very responsible person and I couldn't stand watching him self-destruct. He is the most intelligent, creative person I have ever met and I still love him and feel a deep connection with him, but he constantly evades me. I am very sad that my soulmate left me without even trying to resolve our relationship on this plane. Some insight into this situation would be gratefully appreciated.

M.S.
Lake Tahoe, CA

 When I entered the contact room, Abenda was talking to a bright, cheerful woman who introduced herself as Lady Lonasin. She had this to say: "In London and Vienna, you partied the days and nights away with your beloved. He loved the lifestyle, but even then, you knew it was a setting for destruction. You will get over this sense of fate and the irony of it in time. You know that he could not keep the show going on and on, as he tries to now. This is his karma; you have tried to help, but your influence is no longer a factor. And you are not to worry about this. People will step in to help him take control of his life at the appropriate time.

"In the meantime, you must search your feelings and know that you can be a friend to him but not a partner in self-destruction. You will gain peace of mind, and someday you can work at being his friend again. From your past lives, you will reap happiness in this life. Not everyone is deserving of this. You must look forward to your coming happiness and honor." —**Lady Lonasin**

Abenda added this note: "Drugs are both a cultural gift and a cultural demise. As the gift of science comes to your world, so do those who abuse these gifts. You are to look to the light to follow the goodness of mankind. Destroying the temple of the mind and body has repercussions on earth as well as on your resting time between incarnations. Look for the gifts in all experiences."

Too Shy To Find Love

 Dear Tara: I know that you are very busy, but I just don't know who else to turn to. Here is my problem: I am thirty-six years old. I am told I am a very attractive woman, but I have never done well in relationships with men. I never dated much, and haven't been on a date in ten years.

I consider myself to be a friendly person, but I am also quite shy. The more attracted I am to a man, the shyer I become. I am very lonely and have been lonely for what seems like a very long time.

When I was twenty-five, I briefly considered suicide

because of my loneliness, but I didn't because I had a dream that discouraged me from doing it. I haven't considered suicide again, but I am very depressed about my situation. I have been to a number of psychiatrists and counselors, and none of them could understand why I have any problems with the opposite sex. Please help me. Will I ever have a relationship that lasts longer than two seconds? If you do take this letter to Abenda for her help, when you meditate, could you please say hello to my mother, father and grandparents for me? Also, tell them that I love them and miss them.

J.K.
Long Branch, NJ

A nun with a serene, peaceful face appeared to answer Janice's question: "In a past life, Janice was a prostitute in ancient Rome. After that lifetime, she spent many lifetimes as a nun, cloistered away from the temptations of the flesh, because she felt she needed the discipline. She has brought many strict morals from those lifetimes into this one.

"She doesn't need that kind of discipline anymore, but she is finding it difficult to make the transition to a secular person with a normal sexual/love relationship. She really does want a family, but she doesn't know what to do or how to act.

"All this will change for her very soon—as soon as she gets really straight with herself and gets out to meet men. I'm not much help to her in that department, but I do try to help her meet men. On a subconscious level, she knows I am trying to help her, for she and I spent many lifetimes in the convents together. She will soon

22

meet a good man and she will have babies with him. She mustn't worry." —**Sister Maria Francesca**

Abenda added a quick note: "Janice, you need to acquire a few hobbies to enable you to meet nice men. You have good karma, so relax and give your life a chance!"

Attracted To Wrong Men

Q Dear Tara: I'm sure you must get many letters like mine, but if you can help, I would be so grateful. In this lifetime, I have had four serious relationships, all with incompatible men. The only thing they all had in common was that most people did not get along with them. All of them were mean, rude, immature, and insensitive. All of them had reputations within their own families as being "difficult to get along with."

These were very painful relationships for me. I always ended up feeling that I could do a lot better. In fact, people have always told me that these men were not worthy of me. When I would finally get fed up and end the relationship, each one was sorry to see me go. By the time I left them, they were usually motivated to change for the better, but it would be too late for me because I would have fallen out of love with them. In each case, when I left, I chose another one just like him, or worse.

Why do I keep choosing the same type of man? I married the fourth one, and he's the worst of all. I have paid a heavy emotional price. The only way I kept from having a complete emotional breakdown was to go into therapy. I'm fine now and can hold my own against my soon-to-be ex-husband, but I'm afraid of getting another one with the same or worse characteristics.

Is there a lesson in all of this that I'm missing? I'm basically a strong, positive person who is mentally and emotionally sound. I'm afraid to marry again and have children until I know what's going on. Can you help?

T.V.
Tampa, FL

A **When Abenda called in her guide, I expected to see a sympathetic woman with advice for Tracy. I was surprised to see a big Roman centurion dressed in the typical attire of his era. He smiled as he held out his hand for the pen:** "Tracy, Tracy, you always go for the big, macho types. Maybe that's why I'm your guide. You need to take a stance against being attracted to these cads. You will learn after this divorce. It has not been a fun experience for you. Make sure you remember it so you don't make the same mistakes again.

"In a past life in Rome, you were the emperor's personal scribe. You were always on your toes, serving him, and so he greatly favored you. He was a very spoiled, immature, and selfish person, but you saw him as being macho and powerful. It was not a sexual relationship, so you were never disappointed in your notion of him as wonderful and strong. You must change your perception of how you view men. It is okay to be giving but you must learn to be discerning in your affection and love. It would be wise for you to keep a journal so you can analyze your instincts and feelings. You can always ask me for an accurate insight into a man you're interested in." —**Tironius**

> **Abenda added this note:** "This is a dilemma a lot of people come into the earth plane to experience. Open your heart chakra with pink light and feel oneness with others and with all of life. You will go on and make the right choices. Seek balance, peace and harmony; use this as a mantra to acquire this."

Killed His Wife

Q Dear Tara: For my own peace of mind and personal growth, I would really like to know the karmic relationship, if any, between me and my former wife, Dona. I am in prison because I killed her in a fit of passion and rage. I'm trying desperately to find out why it ended so violently. It was a terrible mistake and now society demands that I pay for my actions.

We had a tumultuous relationship for thirteen years. I loved her very much and she loved me, but our relationship was like a crazy rollercoaster ride. What makes this so tragic is that there had never been any violence between us, only anger, and I hadn't had so much as a traffic ticket in over twenty years before this happened.

My first wife, Dorothy, has attended Dick's seminar on hypnotic regression and has performed several successful regressions. She feels that there is, or was, a karmic connection between Dona and me, but is unable to receive any details.

I've read all the books I've been able to obtain in

these circumstances, but the answers still elude me. I've exhausted all other avenues available to me and I beseech your assistance in helping me to understand what happened between Dona and me to cause such a violent reaction that subsequently placed me in prison. Knowing if such a karmic connection exists would help me greatly in my search for understanding and peace of mind.

D.D.
Tehachapi, CA

A **woman who identified herself as Dona stepped forward to answer this:** "Don, I am fine. I realize you have gone through much sadness as you stayed there to face the consequences of your action. Ours was a riveting and wrathful relationship. I was drawn to your energy intensely, but you wanted to tell me how my life should be run, and I got stubborn and dug my heels in. I know you tried and tried to make our relationship work, we just went through times of turmoil.

"I visit you in prison frequently, but you don't see me or know I'm there. I'm sorry you're so depressed over your circumstances. I've wanted to tell you that everything's okay, I'm okay. I'm so glad to have this opportunity to tell you so, although I know it doesn't really change your situation. I hope the next time we see each other, we will be kinder to each other and release our pain. I may have died on the earth plane, but I feel alive over here. You should not feel so guilty; it was karmic. You must go on with your life and accomplish good things; even in prison, good things can be accomplished by small deeds. Love." **—Dona**

Abenda shook her head and quickly wrote this: "I'm not satisfied. I'd like to call in one of Don's guides or Dona's, and see their past lives together."

A short dark woman with a black lace shawl draped over her head entered the room and sat on the couch. She wrote: "Donald is suffering such immense emotional pain that even Dona goes down to comfort him. He must release his anguish and realize that this was the potential of a lesson he failed. Dona only transformed to this existence, she is essentially alive still. Theirs was a passionate, on-again, off-again romance. They sparked unusual love and hate feelings in each other. Communication between them was usually a blunt, often tactless shouting match instead of calmly sitting down and working things out. Dona was as much at fault in these angry outbursts as Donald. But Donald lost his temper so fiercely that Dona is with us and no longer there on the earth plane. It could easily have been the other way around. Dona would like to see Donald be released, but the prison system in your society is very strict, so he must make the best of it.

"Their past lives together: Dona was a white male slave owner and Donald was her slave. In that life, she worked him very hard. One minute she would show kindness, then cruelty and contempt the next. Donald used to fantasize about killing his master so he could be free of the oppression.

"In another life, Donald was a businessman in the South. Dona was a prostitute he became intrigued with, but she only got close when she wanted to. This was the start of their physical bonding. There were no negative experiences in that life, so at their inter-life council session, they decided to be married in this life and really be together. But they have not yet begun to resolve all the hurt and anger that closeness can bring out. Dona wants Donald to be all he can be, but Donald's subconscious mind only picks up the bossy slave owner. Theirs is a power struggle—who is in control? Once more Donald is in confinement like a slave. He must realize that wisdom erases karma. When he consciously forgives both Dona and himself, then he can go forward in his evolution." —**Brionetta Spinoza**

> **Abenda nodded in satisfaction and added this note:** "Wisdom does erase karma. Because of the karmic bonds we have with others, it is a real problem when we let these negative tendencies enter our lives. Don, you must put a lot of white light protection around you. You will be all right."

Love Turned Sour

Q Dear Tara: There is a situation in my life concerning an ex-lover who has surfaced again through my brother. Here's a brief background sketch: In 1982, I went to Alaska on a two-month working vacation. I took a job as a waitress. I loved Alaska and decided to make it my home. After five months, I met a man and we fell in love the moment our eyes met. At first, the relationship with Waldo was wonderful, but after six months, everything turned sour. He was verbally abusive, jealous and controlling. Within two years, he became physically abusive as well. I left him and returned to California.

But, here's the situation I'm concerned about. My brother Tony went to Alaska in 1989 on a fishing trip. A friend had given him the number of a local fishing guide, who turned out to be Waldo. At that time, I still hadn't fully worked through my feelings about Waldo, so my brother decided to use another fishing guide. In 1991, again my brother planned a fishing trip to Alaska and again Waldo was recommended as a fishing guide by still another friend. My brother and I discussed this, and I told him that I thought we had some very strong karmic ties with Waldo and that he should meet him, but he still didn't do it.

I don't want to stand in the way of my brother's opportunity to work through his karma with Waldo. He keeps showing up in our lives and I think it's time to find out why. Waldo has displayed some psychic powers, but in my opinion, he is a very dark person. I traveled a long way to meet this man and he had a profound effect on my life. All of this is too coincidental not to be predestined. After many years, I was finally able to deal with my feelings for him and have let him go. I am now at peace with my feelings. But I don't want my brother or me to have to meet him again in another life if we can clear this up now.

Is there anything you or your guides can tell me that can help us work out this karmic configuration?

L.B.
Claremont, CA

An old Eskimo dressed in furs and sealskin mukluks stood by the window, waiting patiently for me to finish greeting Abenda. His weathered face creased in a smile as he sat on the couch to write the following: "I believe in the old ways. That is why Linda and Waldo did not take to the mating call. She is a woman of your world, the fast city world, far from nature. Waldo asked me to be his guide and help him go back to the old ways in this lifetime. He asked me to help him learn to live close to the land and water, to experience the realms of beauty with the mountains and clear non-human space surrounding us.

"The past lives that Linda had before with Waldo was on the American Plains as pioneers in the early 1800's. Waldo worked very hard to make a life for them, but Linda complained constantly about the niceties of the civilized life they had left behind. She had been raised a city girl, and she wanted to go back. She and Waldo did not work it out in that lifetime. She was really sorry that it didn't work, and decided to try it again in this lifetime. Instead of the Plains, they were in the great North, very different uncharted land. Again, it did not work out. So Linda has come back to mainstream society.

"Waldo does not resent you as you do him; he wishes he had a partner and that life could've been different between you. As for her brother having contact with Waldo, it is just a very small world." **—Tanaka Sam**

They Let Love Slip Away

Dear Tara: I am very intrigued by your automatic writing column. I'm writing to you to ask you to use your abilities to help me understand my karmic situation.

I have always been a very private individual. I never needed a lot of people around me and wasn't big on dating either, because I always believed that my special person would find me. And he did, eleven years ago. We met at a church convention in a remote mountain resort. We fell in love that night, and dated for two years, even though we lived two thousand miles apart. Finally, we married and I thought we would be happy forever. But somehow, over the next eight years, something went wrong. We are now divorced. Even though we still love each other, we are no longer "in love" with each other.

I believe we had a love unlike anything most people will ever feel in many lifetimes—so pure and innocent and true. I also believe that we have shared this love throughout many lives together, and it pains me to know that we let this love slip away just as we were on the verge of perfecting it. It's been almost a year since I last saw him, and it still hurts to know this great love is gone.

I feel deep in my soul that I will regain this love someday. I must. Everyday, I think about my soulmate and I wonder if he was really my soulmate or just someone to help me get ready for my soulmate. I feel as though my lesson in all this is to learn patience, which I've always had trouble with. I work on it everyday, believing that as soon as I've conquered patience, I will regain this love. Please help me understand why we have allowed this to happen to us. What is my lesson in all of this? I want to love like this again in this lifetime.

D.W.
St. Louis, MO

A young woman clad in shimmering, iridescent robes took the pen to answer Diana: "Diana, I want to say what a pleasure it is to say hello to you and to be able to communicate over this sad problem you find yourself in. We are trying to work it out on this side for you, too. Sometimes you do not appreciate people until they are gone. Your ex-husband really loves you, too, but the problem you have will keep him away until you make a conscious choice to change. Until you open up, his life will go one way and yours another. This issue stems from many past lives.

"Once, in a lifetime in China, you had many children. In fact, that is all you two did—have many, many children. There was no time to really get to know each other because you both had to work very hard to care for your large family. In this life, you desire more contact than merely sexual—you want dreams and conversation, and you don't want to be burdened by too many children or interruptions.

"You also had a life together in England. You were well off because your husband worked very hard to give you the grand lifestyle. In fact, he worked so hard that you never saw him; you didn't even sleep in the same room together. So there was minimal contact, in both the physical and mental sense. Now you are seeking a happy medium between these two lives, but trying to restore the mental, which is communication and becoming true friends. It would be wise to keep a diary of your feelings. Be honest with yourself so you can recognize how to be honest with others. We know it is hard to lose a loved one, especially over something that is essentially trivial. We all learn from and grow with pain. Now is the time to learn and grow." —**Mary Mae**

Soulmate Dumped Her

Q Dear Tara: I would like to know why, after I found my soulmate, he cruelly dumped me? Also, why does the white light I send toward him have the strange effect of making him hate me? I have been tempted to think that the whole soulmate concept is bull, but I would still like to believe that soulmates do exist.

Since my soulmate left me, I have had two boyfriends, but no other relationship can compare to a soulmate relationship. I am so lonely for my soulmate and so confused about this. Can you please help me, or at the very least, tell me what I can do to keep from dying of loneliness? I'm so afraid my soulmate will have nothing to do with me for the rest of my life.

K.
Mesa, AZ

A **Abenda was already writing when I entered the room, so I quietly nodded to the woman waiting patiently on the couch. This is what Abenda wrote:** "Kirra is disillusioned with life and love. A soulmate is a person who gives back 100 percent of your love. If you do not receive as much love as you give in return, you are working with a karmic situation. You can love many people, and in many cases, your love is not reciprocated. If you experience this, you have set up for yourself to learn lessons of the heart. You may have this karma. The first alleviation of karmic relationships is to learn wisdom and overcome fear. You may not appear fearful, but what you chose on the other side manifests as love or the lack of love you find in your life. I will let Anika tell Kirra of her past lives."

Abenda handed the pen and notepad to the woman, who began to write rapidly: "You know that there are many times I have helped you clarify the situation between yourself and your lost love. He is not for you. You must open the picture of the future and see that your love is not enough to save yourself or him. Love is never enough. There must be maturity and respect along with love. Otherwise love is at its very early stages and cannot withstand tests and trials.

"Your love karma with this man includes love ties in an Atlantean lifetime. It was a very open, loving relationship, and you had many children. It was a very happy lifetime. You also had some English lifetimes that were very happy experiences. Your last love experience with him was during an American Indian lifetime. You belonged to warring tribes, and though you loved each other, you both remained loyal to your tribes. So you decided to come together in this lifetime, but again neither is willing to bend.

"Your road in this life isn't as hard as his. You must be strong and trust in your destiny. You have a much better life coming up for you. Open yourself to love and healing. Your past lives have been very positive concerning love; maybe that's why you expect so much from love. But you must first rely on yourself, then you will meet a man to share your life with." —**Anika**

In Love With Her Cousin

Q Dear Tara: I have been so impressed by your column. It has become my favorite part of the *Master of Life WINNERS* magazine. I feel strongly compelled to write to you about a situation in my life.

Twelve years ago, something happened that changed my life. I fell in love with my cousin. (Our common ancestor is my great-grandfather, who is his great, great-grandfather.) The relationship was immediate and intense. We planned to marry, but several family members put pressure on him to abandon the relationship, and he complied. Since that time, we have kept in touch. Although we are separated by great distances, we see each other when we can and have in fact jeopardized current relationships to be together.

I have tried very hard to get over him and put a closure on the relationship, but it never seems to work. It is as though he is a part of me and I'm not sure I could be happy if he were completely out of my life. The love I feel for him is like no other love I have ever had. We are both married now but continue to affirm our love for one another. There is also a very powerful physical attraction between us. I would appreciate any insights you may have concerning this situation—it has been a source of pain and confusion in my life since it began.

C.W.
Kailua, HI

A teenage girl had this to say: "Cathy is worried about her cousin. She didn't want to come in as his cousin, but she was afraid she might not see him again if she didn't. She wanted a tie that would bind them together for life.

"This is because of the last lifetime they shared. They were neighbors in Ireland during the start of the great civil war. They fell in love but it was destined to be unfulfilled. His family was Protestant; hers was Catholic. Her father was involved with the IRA and killed many Protestants. Neither would leave their families but they never forgot their love for each other. I was her best friend, so I know how she suffered.

"Cathy thought this time at least she'd be near him and could always love him unconditionally. And she can love him unconditionally. Concerning their love affair, she must realize her choices and know that love transcends such yearnings. She can have her cake and eat it too, but she must be careful as both families would again be at odds with them. She must learn to turn her thoughts in the direction of writing or arts and crafts. This will give her self-esteem and help her take her mind off the situation." —**Brenda**

Note from Abenda: "The choices we make for ourselves can be hard. You may feel that you don't have this person but he is blood of your blood, life of your life, love and more love. You must count your blessings and look positively on the situation."

She Fears Lover Is Dead

Q Dear Tara: When I saw your automatic writing column, something told me to write to you. I have been living in doubt for six years and need your help. I cannot pursue my "missing person" through normal channels. Please, if you publish this, change our names. I know how ruthless people beyond the law work—our real names could get us hurt.

During the spring of 1986, I had been seeing my lover Michael for five years. Two years before, he had taken an on-the-road job that kept him away most of the time. One day in March, as I said good-bye to him in a parking lot, I somehow knew that I would never see him again. I tried to argue myself out of this feeling—after all, I'd watched him drive away dozens of times before.

He usually called me every two or three days when he was on the road, but this time it was almost two weeks before I heard from him. He sounded scared and told me that someone had tried to kill him twice. Once, by trying to force him off the highway and once by shooting out his tires while he was traveling about ten miles over the speed limit. He said he was going to go underground for a while and told me that he would contact me as soon as possible.

A few weeks later I received an unsigned postcard in his handwriting that said he was okay, but it would still be a while. That was the last time I ever heard from him.

That fall I began having terrifying dreams about Michael. The dreams were always the same. In them, his truck would come to a screeching halt. Then the driver's door would open and Michael would fall out onto the roadway. There were people standing by the side of the road, looking at him, but doing nothing as he lay, dying, in a pool of his own blood. I know in my heart that he is dead, that he died the way I saw it in the dream.

Can you and your guides help me? I have been waiting for him, hoping that my dreams mean nothing, but afraid that they do. It would help me to let go if I could really believe that Michael is dead.

"Frances"

A short, dark man nodded briefly at me then wrote the following: "Michael is gone. Even if he wasn't, how could you take him back after such heartache, no matter what his excuse? When he took that job, he sealed his fate. He was smuggling drugs and got too far involved. He knew it was dangerous but thought he was being careful and nothing would happen to him. But he took too many chances and the people he worked for decided they would be better off without him.

"To spare your feelings would punish you much more. You need to get a grip on your life and let him go with unconditional love. Michael never wanted you to be unhappy. In fact, it hurts his karma more deeply to think that you are wasting your life. He knows he should have warned you that he was involved in something dangerous. It was his risk, but he felt like he knew what he was doing at the time.

"You are a wonderful person; he thought so too. Open yourself and you will find a wonderful life filled

with happiness." —**Frank Brentano**

Abenda added this at the bottom of the page:
"You know, life isn't always what you had hoped for, but you tried very hard to be good and truthful to someone who wasn't entirely truthful in return. You can breathe deeply and relax, surrounding yourself with white light. Let go of chaos with the exhale, and inhale peace. You must learn to trust again, to trust yourself to make the right choices, to have love and give it freely. Work at open communication and honesty. Your life will run smoothly from now on. You don't want any more surprises and that is fine, just open yourself to experience joy."

She Is In Love With A Gay Man

 Dear Tara: I hope you can answer this question for me. I am thirty-seven years old. When I was fifteen, I became involved with a married man We had a child and were together for three years. When we broke up, a man I barely knew moved in with me. After we had a child, we got married and had two more children. He was a very abusive man, and our marriage finally ended when my husband stabbed me. That was two years ago.

After the divorce, I got a job. Through my employer, I met a man that I felt an immediate attraction to. He felt it too, and we became fast friends, going everywhere together. There is just one problem—he is gay. We have never had sex, although we have a very sexual relationship and spend our nights together.

His sexual orientation doesn't really bother me; I feel like we are married spiritually. In fact, our ever-deepening friendship is causing him to end his current relationship with his lover. Although I love him unconditionally, it has not been easy for me as I have four children and a maniac ex-husband who has threatened to kill anyone involved with me. Though my ex-husband is in prison for stabbing me, he will be released later this year.

Because I love my gay friend and won't sleep with anyone else, my sex life is nil. I want to have sex with him, but I live without it. He says he loves me and wishes he weren't gay, but he is and I'll just have to accept it. My friends think I need to get a real life with a man who can give me what I deserve—even he says that, but I can't give him up. I feel like we are connected and belong together.

So, this is my question: Are we karmically connected? Did I hurt him so badly in another life that he is punishing me in this one? Although I love him, I would have to say that he is not a wonderful man. He is an alcoholic, and he abuses me mentally and physically. He is also very jealous of me. Yet I just want to love away his need to hurt me, and am doing my all to continue to love him unconditionally.

C.M.
Tampa, FL

 Automatic writing received: "Your relationship with your gay friend is a safe one. He tries to be as much of a friend as he can be for you. You want more, but he can only be who he is.

"You need to clarify your real needs. You can have

this man for a best friend while you look for a boyfriend. You can have many friends; don't give others ultimatums in life over your lack of security and self-esteem. You must work on this. Protect yourself from all negative influences. If you are unhappy in your situation, then you can change it. No more excuses. You can do it.

"Your husband is so full of anger. He is a dangerous man and is not to be taken lightly. You have sought to relinquish your burdens from past lives. He was among the men you commanded in a past life. You took them into battle, knowing that most of them would die. You died with them, but you have held on to the guilt you felt for leading them to their deaths. You must let them go. Your ex-husband is truly not sane anymore. He has been a warrior in so many lifetimes that he sees everyone as the enemy. You must protect yourself from him. Your children are in no danger from him, but you certainly are. He needs medical help very badly. At times he seems rational, but the surges of irrationality come over him when he sees you." —**Harold Reinford**

> **Abenda had this to say:** "Please do not take your ex-husband lightly. You are learning to work through your dilemmas in life. Are you currently in counseling? It would be very helpful for you to be able to express your needs to someone who is trained to help. They could help you through these times. I know you like challenge—it makes you feel vibrant and alive, but you must make it work for you and not against you."

He's Gay, In Love With A Straight Man

 Dear Tara: I know you probably get thousands of letters, but I'm hoping and praying that you can take the time to help me.

I am twenty-nine years old and gay. I am in love with my best friend, Chris, who is a married man. He's four years younger than me. We horse around a lot and do some things that even best friends don't do. To make things even more interesting, his wife is in love with me. She's not happy with her marriage, but she told me once that she stays with him so she can continue to see me.

I've never told either one of them that I am gay, although I think Chris suspects. I know he has certain feelings for me, but he can't deal with them, and we're both too scared to make the first move. We call each other several times every day and see each other every evening. In fact, I see more of him than his wife does.

I want to know if your guides can tell me if Chris really does love me? When will he be willing to talk about his true feelings? This situation has been ongoing for over two years, and it's really having an effect on me. If you can please help me, I would be ever so thankful.

R.R.
Philadelphia, PA

 Abenda was in the room when I entered. Soon, an older, scholarly-looking man entered. This is what he wrote: "Roger, there are indeed deep feelings between you and this man. You have been in love with him many times before, but in this lifetime, you have a problem, since he is not gay.

Even though he is very sensitive, he has no intention of being either gay or bisexual. There are many couples who are bisexual, but not these two. He doesn't mind that his wife loves you because he knows you are not really interested in her.

"You must compromise your feelings and realize that even if you can't have him as a sexual partner, you do have him as a very dear friend. You must realize that you chose a married heterosexual man as the focus of your fantasies. Be extremely careful and begin to look safely for a real boyfriend, as you need to start expressing your love in a positive environment.

"In a past life in Greece, you were a page for a very wealthy, politically powerful man. He was your lover and benefactor. You were very loyal and good, but when you grew older, he replaced you with a younger boy. You were very hurt; this manifests today in your need to find security within a relationship. You have frequently made fun of permanence in relationships, but it is something you deeply desire for yourself.

"You have good intentions. Be strong and brave. All choices happen so you can learn and grow." —**Heinrich Bernhardt**

> **Abenda added this note:** "You mustn't despair. All trials on the road of life happen for a reason, and within that reason, your karma and dharma exist. You must remember that every painful thought helps you to obtain awareness. Wisdom erases karma. You must count your blessings."

Chapter Two

Family Relationships

Some of our most important learning opportunities are with our families. These relationships have the potential to positively or negatively mark an individual for the rest of their life. There has recently been much talk about dysfunctional families, but that is just a new buzzword for something that has been around ever since we first began incarnating on the earth plane. The people with whom we are meaningfully involved in this life have shared many past lives with us.

I have heard a lot of people comment that they don't choose their families, but they do choose their friends. Actually, they did choose their families at the inter-life council. At that time, the circumstances of their birth, their family life, future mates and directions were chosen. You picked your parents, friends, and lovers ... even your enemies. I don't mean to say there is no free will during the lifetime, because there is. You could say it is like a card game—your karma deals the hand, but you choose how you play it. On the other side, we sometimes choose to deal ourselves very difficult hands but then are reluctant to play the cards we've dealt.

I asked for some input from Rod Invergordon and Abenda about family relationships.

Rod Invergordon wrote: "Family can provide many karmic tests. Even though we don't always get the love and attention we aspire to in early years, we can learn by the hurt we experience. As adults we can choose not to renew the pain and sadness we felt when we were younger. Pain is a greater teacher than joy. When we feel joy, we get caught up in it and don't strive harder to achieve our goals.

"In regard to family, tell the truth *to yourself.* Do not lie to yourself or about others; this will allow you to see your family in a true light. If your father or mother treats you badly, you must realize that you are fulfilling the debts of a previous lifetime. How should you react to mental or physical abuse? It is a hard question to answer; the cycle is vicious, but you must let go of the negativity because that is your primary purpose on the wheel of fate. Ask yourself the right questions and live fully with a good heart, for you will reap the rewards."

From Abenda: "With all relationships, you must gain a certain level of affinity or the relationship may not fulfill your needs. This is very true with families. As an example, you feel you should love your mother, but the feelings just aren't there. But if you are consciously acting in a positive way, then you have nothing to worry about. You must search for other feelings among your brothers and sisters in humanity. Even if you do not feel the love of another, you can feel oneness with your community, nature, or your home. Seek out other passions in life. Most importantly, you are not to blame anyone else for your lack of life. You, and only you, have the power to make your life the way you want it to be.

"You can have passion or mediocrity, it is up to you to choose your paths. Your family, lovers and friends are here to learn also. If you don't have what you want, it's time to explore the purpose of your relationships, which can provide you with karmic understanding. Ask yourself, 'What can I learn about myself through this relationship? How can I act with unconditional love?' We are one people, one world, one universe, we are of one light. The answers are within your Higher Self."

She Can't Give Love Freely

 Dear Tara: I get goose bumps when I read your column in the magazine. I just know you can help me find out why I'm unable to love freely. I guard my privacy and my space fiercely, although it doesn't seem to do much good. My belief in reincarnation helps me to know that there are reasons for this. I'm sure if I knew, I could understand and deal with it better. I come from a very unloving home. Only one aunt showed us any caring. I never bonded with my parents and can't seem to bond with my husband either. I am almost sixty and have been married more than forty years. I had a very self-centered, self-absorbed mother who took me out of school when I was sixteen so I could keep house for her. I married early to get away from this and my husband is a very jealous, over-protective and tough man. Both husband and mother have mellowed over the years, but now my mother is living with us. Each is extremely judgmental and always has to be "right."

Please ask your guides why this happened, that I can't give love freely to them, and how to cope with the years ahead as my husband retires. I do feel free to love two sisters, a brother, my daughter and grandchildren, but others, especially the mother and husband, are very difficult to show love to.

A.C.
South Bend, IN

*A*s I entered the contact room, Abenda was pouring tea for a middle-aged man and a young girl. The man wrote first: "In your last life, you were never able to get away from your husband. He was overly possessive and very insecure; he did not want you to be seen by others or to have a life of your own. You resented him very much. He is your mother in this life. In the inter-life council, you decided to come back and try it again, only without resentment. So, in this life, you cleaved to her and it made her very happy.

"You are not to despair over wanting to be free and idealistic and have a mind of your own. This is your God-given right. To break this cycle, you must forgive your husband and your mother, and start preparing your life for changes. You are not to accept fate as you think it will turn out; you are to gain wisdom, independence and fortitude. Be free." **—John B. Holmby**

Abenda added this note: "It is hard to fulfill our karma with others. You deserve much out of life, as do all others of your gender. But sometimes our karma limits our actions. First, you must think through all aspects of life, and then take the most positive action. One thing you can do is to help your mother find interests in life other than controlling you. Maybe she could become involved in some women's social clubs, or get a pet. I am referring to this in a general state, as I know you know best what your mother likes and needs.

"John was right—forgiveness is the first step for you. I have another guide here who will go further back into your past-life lineage to help you understand."

The young girl then wrote: "In a past life, you were an Italian heiress. You had a fabulous life, but it was built on the lives of others. We were only there to serve you. You demanded that your interests come before everything else in our lives, so you wouldn't allow us to marry or have children. You even required all of us to adhere to the Catholic religion. When I tried to tell you that we were happy to serve you but we wanted to have our own lives, you threw me out in the street. So, in this life, you have had to experience the total domination that we felt. I came to tell you these things so you would understand, but I wish for no more contact." **—Marta**

John added a final note: "You are not to be troubled over these times; you can have good times in the future, but you must break the habits now. Learn to take and learn to give." **—John Holmby**

She's Resisting 'What Is'

 Dear Tara: In one of your columns, you told someone, "It is your resistance to what is that causes your suffering." I wish you could further explain this. I have spent a very long time trying to rid myself of the resistance I feel toward my father and other members of my family, but I'm not having much success. I know that the more I resist them, the worse they get, yet when I try letting my guard down, they jump right in for the kill. I know I am drawing this to me, yet I don't seem able to stop it.

D.F.
Kalamazoo, MI

An English gentleman wrote the following:
"You have needed to let go of your father's ways for a very long time, mentally letting go of the need to be right. He is very passionate about the things he says, which stir ancient resentments within you. You are to send him white light and unconditional love, and understand that his truth is not your truth. You are to let that go. Even though you haven't accomplished this yet, you continue to learn and grow. His inability to listen to your views gives you insight on your motives and desires in life, and you start to see the pattern of learning. When you fully accept this, you will go on and finish your negative karma. He will resist you less and you can finish the healing process that you started long ago.

"In a Japanese past life, you were a traditional woman, with bound feet, married into a family of very dominating powerful men. Your present-life father was then your father-in-law. The women in the household were meek, never allowed to state an opinion. Thus, your father continues to not listen to your views. He has a lineage of many Eastern past lives that had this way of looking at women. He is learning, but you are the one being taught, so do not take it so hard. Just flow with the circumstances. Find your voice and calmly state your opinion. Know that they matter. You matter." **—Henrich Fallows**

Abenda took the notepad and added this note: "The statement, 'It is your resistance to what is that causes your suffering' is self-explanatory. You resist your father and you suffer as a result. The idea is to stop resisting what you cannot change—unalterable realities. Your father won't change. If you're going to remain in his life, you'll suffer until you accept him as he is and stop resisting him.

"You know that you are smart and strong; show how strong you can be by learning from all situations requiring patience. Compromise and keep the peace. Your father is your spark of creation; he must fulfill his karma even as you fulfill yours. You are one."

War With Ex-Husband

 Dear Tara: About eight years ago, I underwent a long and brutal divorce proceedings. Ultimately, I was awarded custody of our two children and our home. Since then, the relationship between us has been more than strained. Physically, we have not seen each other, except once or twice at a distance. We don't speak, except on rare occasions. I always feel as if I'm being manipulated and I usually end the conversation by hanging up. The kids have had an especially hard time with all of this.

The person most affected is my son. He's had a very difficult time at school and we've gone through years of counseling. He told me he wanted to live with his father, so after some counseling, I let him stay with his father for a more extended summer vacation. It wasn't long before my ex-husband, his new wife and my son had all had their fill of each other, and he returned home. I thought this episode was behind me until recently, when things started to heat up again.

Three weeks ago, the District Attorney's office collected a large amount of back child-support from my ex-husband. The next time my son went to visit, he never returned. I was served with legal papers granting my ex-husband temporary custody. In order for the temporary custody to be granted, my son had to give an affidavit saying he was being abused and crimes were being committed in his presence. None of this is true.

I want the pain to stop. You wouldn't believe the power struggles and manipulations that have gone on here. Do my ex-husband and I have some long, black history of hurting one another? Is this why he's using our son as a tool to hurt me? How are the children involved and how can I stop this cycle? I don't see any resolution and am afraid this will go on and on. Please help!

S.M.
Seattle, WA

A woman named Katherine wrote this: "Susan, we know you are going through a rough time right now, but you are to flow with the changes that occur in your life. Send light and love into your emotional turmoil. Your son has made a choice and is not to be sought at this time. You are to love him from afar and send him notes and presents. Release your anger over the past and those situations beyond your control. It is time to allow your old marriage to rest amongst the dust, and to heal all wounds. You can send unconditional light and love to your ex, for you are not to have this emotional attachment. You are to release the negative attachment and make it a neutral arrangement. You have a new destiny coming, so you must stabilize and put fun in your life again. You can do it." **—Katherine Hanswonds**

> **Abenda then wrote this:** "It is very hard to let go when there are strings attached to the heart. If you need to fret and worry, you can, but this doesn't help you. All will be well in time. Open the door for your son to easily step in to love his mother again. Let go of the past and send him love."

Why Is Daughter Autistic?

 Dear Tara: Please ask your guides why my daughter was born deaf and mildly autistic. She will be thirty-four in June. She lives with us and is functional—she works as a data entry clerk and drives her own car. She will always have to live in a protected environment—either with us or in a group home. I am fifty-seven and my husband is fifty-nine, and we had always wanted to buy a trailer and see America when my husband retires in three years. But our daughter is a problem—none of my family can stay with her and we don't know what else to do.

J.R.
Atlanta, GA

 A middle-aged man moved forward to answer Joy's question: "Joy, you need to relax and work through these blocks that make up the difficult road of life. You have this autistic deaf daughter, and even though this has been a great burden on you, you must turn your mind to the rewards. Your daughter came into this life to clean a karmic slate with you, and she is trying to advance for future lives. This was your goal, too, when you planned this life before you were born. But you have forgotten this agreement.

"You need to know that you shared a life as siblings in a wealthy Victorian family, but you both handled that lifetime so badly that you incurred a lot of negative karma. Both of you were irresponsible, drunken and abusive to others. You both felt this life would pay for that life of dissipation and that you could restore yourselves for exciting, prosperous incarnations again.

"Soon, it will be important to make proper decisions for your daughter. If she is put into an institution, make sure you monitor it carefully and keep close ties. You deserve a life, too. Life is not really easy for anyone, but it can get easier if you set your mind in positive channels. This does not mean unrealistic expectations. If there is sunshine, enjoy the sun. If there is rainfall, enjoy the rain. Be in the moment." **—William Forthright**

An Orphan's Past

Q Dear Tara: I am eighteen years old and have been living with my American parents for about eleven years. They adopted me when I was seven years old. I would like to have a better relationship with them, especially with my mom. It seems that she is never satisfied. We argue a lot. It hurts me to constantly fight with her and Dad. They never show me that they care about me, but despite all the fights and disagreements, I still love them. Can you or Abenda help me find out why we have such a poor relationship?

Also, if possible, can you tell me why my birth parents left me at the doorstep of an orphanage home in Korea? The orphanage has no records about who they are. I've always wondered why they left me. I do remember an old couple that came several times and tried to take me away, but the people at the home wouldn't let them. These people were total strangers to me and I was scared of them. I remember hiding in a corner with the other kids sheltering me so the old couple wouldn't see me. I was terrified every time they came to the home. I wonder if they could have been my grandparents? Why was I afraid of them if they were?

A.H.
Patterson, NJ

A **An old Oriental man wrote this:** "Before you were born, you knew that you would go to America. You also knew that your early life would be hard. In the life before this one, you had lost your parents in the concentration camps during the Holocaust. After several months of starvation and cruelty, you died there. Your last thoughts were of freedom. On the other side, you decided that parents were of no real importance in this life as long as you were in a land of freedom and opportunity. Now you have this chance and you have what you want in this regard, so you want the love of the parents also. They seem to hold you back now because they want to hang onto the sad little girl they rescued. You must give them your love and understanding. You know what you must do academically and educationally and your adoptive parents will be very proud of you.

"As for the old couple you saw at the orphanage, they were not your grandparents, though they pretended to be. They visited orphanages throughout Korea to select young children who they then sold to the underworld. The older children knew this, and protected you. That was not your karma. As for your birth parents, it was odd circumstances why they could not keep you. Just send them love and light, and know you chose not to be held back by your birthplace or circumstances. I must also tell you that you will accomplish much, because you get along with a crowd and you know how to stand up for yourself. You have been around an education in the people you have drawn into your life. You will do well; it is your destiny." **—Lin Wu Chong**

> **Abenda wrote this:** "My dear child, you have the whole world in front of you. You will have a good life from now on, but you must always pick the high road and travel it with honesty and dignity."

Past Relationship With Mother

Q Dear Tara: I would like to know about the relationship between my mother and me in previous lives. I think I must have wronged her terribly, because in this life she has been extremely cruel to me. She tortured me when I was growing up. Once she almost killed me. Four years ago, she kidnapped my children and I don't know where they are.

To the rest of the world, she is very kind and giving. She has always acted in a loving and caring way toward my brother, who is ten years younger than me. I don't know why it is just me that she has singled out in this world to hate, unless it is karma from another time. You say that wisdom erases karma, and I long for that wisdom. Can you help me? I need to find my children and get on with my life.

R.P.
San Bernardino, CA

 A woman named Alberta wrote this: "Robin, I know you feel full of despair over your mother's cruelty. You came into this life to work out positive karma with her, but instead you feel it has gotten worse. Your mother is a borderline personality who means well, but it has to be her way or not at all. She has taken the children because she felt it was for your own good. The problems you were experiencing could have been worked out without resorting to such drastic measures, but that is the way your mother is. Your personalities clash and this brings out the worst in her. She is okay with the kids, though, so don't worry. They are being raised the same strict way you were, but you should know that your children chose this before they entered this lifetime. They knew their grandmother and you were going to have problems. You will eventually find them and patch up your relationship with your children. Your mother will fall to the wayside, sickened by loss. Let go and do not feed negativity, for some people live in a hell of their own making. Do not be afraid to ask for help. Many people are keeping an eye out for your children. In these past few years, you have learned some valuable lessons about being more responsible and caring.

"Abenda has asked me to tell you about your past lives with your mother and children. In an Italian lifetime, your mother was your child. You had three other children besides her, but you would not care for them. She was the oldest and took responsibility for their care. She took them into the streets to beg and look for food. Eventually, they all left you. So, you see, your mother is only the product of your past lineage of lifetimes together. Deep down, she still does not trust you. Have you earned her trust in this lifetime? If so, or if not, you now know where this pattern stems from. You can let go of this with love and start to rebuild your life. Mentally draw your children back to you. Eventually, they will respond. You need to forgive your mother, along with yourself." **—Alberta Alberghetti**

> **Note from Abenda:** "Robin, you need to contact the police and organizations dealing with this kind of case. Get them to start looking for your children through the school system, immunization records, etc. Try to find some clues as to where they are. Did she cut ties with your brother or old friends? Do you know where she might be but are afraid to come face to face with her wrath? Search your emotions."

Grandson's Night Terrors

 Dear Tara: My daughter and grandson live with me, as well as my son. My grandson Jordan began having trouble sleeping through the night when he turned three years old. He feels very insecure and wants someone there. In only a few months, it has progressed to the point where one of us actually has to lie down with him until he falls asleep. We can't leave even then, because if he awakens and no one is there, he screams and cries until one of us gets in bed with him again. I can feel his fear and it is overwhelming.

In doing some research of my own, I discovered that I was his mother in a past life. I had drowned when he was three years old. I am wondering if this could be the cause of his fear? Also, how should we handle this problem so he can find peaceful sleep at night so we can keep our sanity?

I would be interested in your insight. So many children have problems sleeping, and we have such strict guidelines in our society about how parents are supposed to lovingly but firmly keep them in their own beds. Is this the best course to help them deal with fear? Standing firm while they scream in their room alone does not have a very comforting ring when I look at the possibility of a past-life reason behind this fear.

L.H.
Phoenix, AZ

A **A man named Tom was present to answer Lynette's question:** "This relates to several lifetimes: Jordan was once a large landowner with many people in his employment. He got sick when he was older and some of the people stole from him—possessions, even land deeds. His family tried to protect him during those bedridden years when he depended on them for assistance in all matters. They comforted him, and he wanted to return again to this 'family.' In this life, he is the youngest and will one day care for them.

"In another shared past life, Lynette, Jordan and two other family members were brothers, enslaved by invaders and forced to row a huge wooden ship. When the ship landed, they were separated and never saw each other again. The group of four also incarnated together as children in a large Hungarian family. Their father died and times were hard, but the four pitched in and helped each other work the family farm. They were successful because they worked as a team.

"Jordan's night terrors are the accumulated fears of past separations. Until the age of six or seven, the past

and present can sometimes seem as one. Dreams inten-
sify the fearful past. But they are once again together in
a group. They should offer the assurance of security.
Know that they are all destined to love and to be together. Cherish the connections. Jordan has a generous
heart for the family and is a true blessing. They will all
see this as time passes." **—Tom Flankins**

> **Abenda added this note:** "All is well with your
> family. You are blessed with love in this lifetime. Let
> go of your ailments; cast them away and enter the
> light. Live fully among your family."

Looking For Past-Life Link

Q Dear Tara: My fourteen-year-old stepson has
some behavioral problems. He does poorly in
school and is a chronic liar. He and his older
sister, who is less difficult, have lived with us permanently for the last seven years. I feel a great deal of
animosity toward their 'mother'—I don't feel she de-
serves the title! I am curious about my past-life associa-
tions with my stepchildren and their mother. Can you
offer any explanation or advice?

**M.G.
Los Angeles, CA**

A **A man named Frank wrote this response:**
"In your last life, you were a girl who was abandoned by her mother in a big city. A woman,
who is your stepdaughter in this life, took you in; your
stepson was her husband. He did not like having you
around and was jealous of your friendship with his wife.

You and she got along very well and it infuriated him. He would storm out of the house and get drunk in the bars. In this life, your stepdaughter still feels close to you, but there are problems because the man in the past life (your stepson now) still feels jealous of your relationship.

The only thing you can do is send your stepson and stepdaughter light and love; show them acceptance. Both children are extremely anxious and fearful. On a superconscious level, they are afraid they are not loved, as their mother in this lifetime rejected them. That is their karma with their mother, which is extremely painful. She was the mother who abandoned you in a past life, which is why you have such negative thoughts about her ability to be a mother. All of you have karma with each other from that life and are continuing to work through it in this life.

"It is time to forgive and let go. Alleviate any further fear-based emotions. To help overcome this negativity, the three of you, or at least the children, should write down their feelings for their mother. Without anyone reading these writings, they should be burnt ceremonially. This helps to release the negative energy. There is hope; they are only teenagers. Give them the best that you can." **—Frank Livingston**

Abenda added this short note: "You are on the road to success with this situation. With love you can overcome many difficulties. Know that you are loved."

She Asks For Fairness

Q Dear Tara: As a child I was very responsible and mature (self-controlled); as an adult I am no different. While I rarely lie, I am, or try to be, tactful. I am considerate of others' privacy and feelings. My parents were abusive physically, mentally and emotionally. The best treatment I received from them was when I was treated as a non-person. At eight years old, I was doing all of the housework but they never recognized my goodness. My mother's threat that Santa Claus could see my every move was greeted with private thoughts that at least he could see how good I was.

In my work I am surrounded by people who lie and cheat the company. They whine loudly when they are busy and because of it are treated with much more respect, generosity and appreciation than I am. My skills are above average and my attitude has been positive, and yet I have been treated very shabbily by people who I have treated only as I would be treated.

Whenever a situation comes down to whether I am to be believed or the wrongdoer is to be believed, the wrongdoer is believed. This was my experience even in school. It seems as though this planet is inhabited by primitive people who rule others by their tempers. Our society is a lonely one, with people seeking out those who would entertain them. People don't select their friends on the basis of their character or lack of it. The most cruel, egocentric individual may be one of the most popular, if he/she is "entertaining" and reveals all of his/her personal life to others. I am a private person who prefers to select my friends rather than have anyone foist themselves upon me. But I do ask for fairness. I know this world is not fair, but I cannot accept that.

Why hasn't my integrity and my goodness been recognized in this lifetime? I'm like the cactus flower, I don't need a lot of nurturing. However, when I have performed or behaved well, I don't expect to be treated badly or blamed for the sins of others. Your explanation would be appreciated.

S.W.
San Francisco, CA

A tall, white-haired man dressed in ancient-looking robes wrote the following through my hand: "You had a life as a barber and you cut hair only in styles that you thought looked good on the person. You always got your way because the townspeople didn't have anywhere else to go. Just as you felt you knew what was best with hairstyles, you now feel your view is the correct one. In this life it is difficult for you to compromise, but it is time you learned to relax and accept others as they are, not as you think they should be. If you begin to open your heart chakra, others will respond in turn." **—Shushkioni-langren**

Abenda added this: "Sandra will be upset by this for she doesn't see herself as someone who needs to be right and wants to control. If she is willing to project a positive attitude, her life will dramatically change and others will cease to bother her. She'll even make lasting friendships among co-workers. The way she is now, if she were to change employment, the same situation will develop in the new job unless she changes her attitude."

A Sisterly Problem

Q Dear Tara: Even as children, my older sister and I did not get along very well. We are now in our late sixties, have little communication and live in different states. She yells at me because I don't often visit our aged mother who lives with her; yet whenever I do, there is always a confrontation. So I stay away, but I do call and write my mother.

I've written my sister, offering to bury the hatchet and start being friends. I get no answer. I don't hate her, but I cannot say I have love for her. She is a person who just happens to be my sister.

Can you give me any insight to this. Is there anything I can do to correct it?

J.C.
Rochester, NY

 Abenda brought a woman named Louella, who said she knew Joanna in a past life. She wrote the following: "Joanna does try, but her sister has no interest in establishing a friendship. Actually, they are both quite happy to stay away from each other. Her sister doubts herself. At this point, it is a conditioned response and she is afraid to change. Joanna needs to try to be unconditional in her love for her sister and her mother, who is in a position of being the child to the daughter.

"Their shared past lives provide a mutual support system. The sister doesn't like to take care of the mother, but that has been their trade-off for many lifetimes. The sister is afraid that no one will take care of her, yet she fears being a burden so she pushes people away.

"The next time her sister yells, Joanna needs to re-mind herself not to take it personally. It is simply what her sister does in response to past experiences. If Joanna can let it go, she will have passed an important karmic test. We are here for her." —**Louella**

Note from Tara: After this response ran in my *Master of Life WINNERS* magazine column, Joanna wrote me, saying: "I feel that Louella is one hundred percent correct in her answer. I realize that the sister/mother relationship is their karmic situation. I will be working on letting go and sending unconditional love. Thank you for easing me."

Mother Is Unaccepting of Son's Homosexuality

 Dear Tara: I am a twenty-one-year-old homo-sexual college student attending college in New York, majoring in advertising and communica-tion arts.

My father recently died of a heart attack, and I'm writing to you because I would like your opinion as to how his death might relate to my karma with my mother. Both my parents knew I was gay. However, my father accepted it and understood it better than my mother, who is still alive.

My father was always open with me about life and metaphysics, despite our strict Catholic upbringing. My father, older brother, and I even visited psychics to-gether. A few months ago, a psychic told me I have a fine life to look forward to: good health, a loving relationship and a successful career in Manhattan. However, the psychic also sensed that my mother was troubled about my being gay, and suggested that I keep working on her to help her understand and accept my lifestyle.

Do you sense that my father died before my mother as an opportunity for me to karmically resolve the situation with mother?

P.B.
New York City, NY

Abenda was in our contact house, along with Patrick's father and a young man who said he was Patrick's guide. Patrick's father was so glad to be able to make contact with his son that it took a few minutes before he could actually write. When he was in control, this is what he wrote: "I didn't mean to leave my boy with thoughts of insecurity. Yes, you and your mother had a few problems on this subject, but she loves you very much. She just has pangs of guilt that somehow she is responsible for the way you are. She goes over and over in her mind what she might have done differently. Of course, I'd try to say a kind word now and then to her, not to get pressured about these things. But she is just not that sort of person. She probably won't ever come around, but she will always love Patrick. So it's a subject they should try to avoid and find other avenues of interest.

"Patrick, I want you to know I am calm and serene. I feel as though I am truly free and life is more of an adventure than ever. I want you to have a good life, to be safe and to study. I also want you to know that I check in at midnight to make sure you're okay. I will try to make contact with you in your dreams. I love you, Pat." **—Dad**

The young man who identified himself as Patrick's guide had this to say: "Pat was always meant to be gay. He has a lot of karma with his mother. She was also his mother in ancient times. She was a prostitute and he had to endure the thought of many men having her body. She loved him and didn't know any other way to feed her son. One day he left and didn't return until she was much older. He cared for her until her death.

"They were also orphans in early America in the Midwest. They only had each other, and even though life was very hard, they found ways to stay together. In many other lives, they have not gotten along, but they stay together as a family, no matter what."

Abenda added this note: "Homosexuality, as a lifestyle choice, is often a way to generate rejection for the experiences that will result. When rejection occurs, karma is created and dispersed. Patrick could benefit by relating his mother's disapproval of his gay lifestyle to his own disapproval of her lifestyle as a prostitute in ancient times. You need to stop the cycle in this lifestyle. The way to resolve it once and for all is through total acceptance of the other as they are, without expectations or blame."

Note from Tara: After this response ran in my *Master of Life WINNERS* magazine column, Patrick wrote to me, saying: "When he was alive, he always told me the same things you got in automatic writing—to 'be safe and study,' and that he checks in with me at midnight—I felt his presence go through me as an emotional rush or force. It was unlike anything I've ever experienced."

Chapter Three
Social Relationships

Your life on earth is entwined with many others—no one lives in a vacuum, unless they have chosen to be a hermit. Yet some of the greatest pain in the letters I receive is not about relationships but the lack of them. So many people feel lonely and unloved, or they experience problems with shyness and fear of rejection that lead them to isolate themselves from others.

Yet you should know you are never, ever alone in life. You have guides and Masters who are always with you, ready to teach and counsel you. Even at the moment of death, where no living friend or family can accompany you, your guides are with you. I asked Abenda and Rod Invergordon for their views on this subject, and this is what they had to say:

Rod Invergordon wrote: "The earth plane is where you learn of joy, pain and fear. Love is joy, sorrow is pain, loneliness is fear. How can you be alone with so many entities surrounding you? Only you can erect barriers—barriers blocking love, creating pain and fear. These barriers are maintained by many earth people to shield themselves. You must mentally remove the barriers and open yourself to experience others and life. You can draw in people who will want to share your light and aura by simply opening to them. This is the first step to joy. Karmically, you attract others of a similar vibration; but not everyone you contact shares karma with you. Reach out; don't wait."

Abenda wrote: "Society is full of people who fear becoming involved. This can be overcome by realizing that everyone feels isolated and lonely at times—all humans have experienced all emotions at one time or another on their soul's journey. Not all people come into life to experience devotion and passion but you will ideally open to relationships that allow you to resolve your karma and fulfill your dharma. Lack of passion is a lack of living; everyone has at least one gift to offer the world, though some people hide their gifts and the world never benefits from them."

Why Am I Shy?

Dear Tara: I am profoundly shy around people I don't know. I become very uneasy when I have to talk to others. I also have a stutter, which prevents me from being confident of myself. This all started when I was in kindergarten. My teachers also noted on my report cards that I didn't socialize and play with others. Anything you can tell me would be appreciated; this shyness has prevented me from having any kind of a social life.

S.S.
San Antonio, TX

Abenda appeared in my contact room with a young girl who seemed very shy and hesitated to write her answer.

Abenda wrote first: "Your guide is as shy as you are. It is okay to desire friendship and laughter. I am holding your guide's hand now as she is terribly afraid of others. I will send someone to help your guide, so she can help you to help yourself. On a subconscious level, you know that this is what you chose for your life. But don't worry, you can overcome this karma. Relax and start telling yourself that you deserve all the joy and goodness that life has to offer. This is true, you do deserve this. I will ask your guide to write of your past lives together and also other past lives of yours where you set up this configuration. Remember, you're here on earth to overcome this karma. Be brave; love is always the answer."

Abenda finally convinced Sojiel's guide to write this: "We have been together in many lifetimes; that is why I am your guide in this lifetime. We died in Nazi Germany together. We were in the Resistance together, and when they caught us they tortured us until we died. That life was to balance an earlier life when we were soldiers in the Civil War. We were Rebels, and we tarred and feathered then hung any escaped slaves we caught. We have paid for that life; we are no longer guilty.

I am always your friend and love you as a very dear friend; I just wasn't strong enough to return to earth. The lifetime during World War II scarred us both. I do not trust others, and I know you are scared of their motives, too. I am sorry that it is I who must help you and that you feel so alone. I just couldn't come back to earth to be your friend in this lifetime. You chose to reincarnate quickly and work through your problems. But even though you don't see me or feel me, I am always with you. You are really never alone. I will try and give you more confidence and trust, so that you can have other really good friends. This would please me as I know you are very strong and can overcome feeling alone. I am glad to talk to you, I hope to be able to talk to you again. I love you, my friend." **—Michaela**

> **Abenda added this note:** "You are to seek out others and get counseling if necessary. You lack trust; that is okay, many others lack trust also. Don't allow your shyness to get in the way of some happiness."

Wants To Be Wife and Mother

 Dear Tara: I have been very impressed with your column and I hope you can help me with a major issue in my life.

I am thirty-five years old, and although I want to be married and have children more than anything else in the world, I have not found anyone who wants to share his life with me in that way. I have used many of your tapes on attracting love, but they haven't helped. I realize that I must have some kind of a barrier or block to getting what I want most in my life. Did I somehow choose to experience this or is there a past-life reason? Any information you can give me regarding this matter will be greatly appreciated.

L.G.
La Mesa, CA

A radiant young woman sat down to write this reply: "Lori, you are a very kind and considerate person, but you have not assertively sought a relationship. You are shy, so most men have thought you weren't interested. You must make yourself go out and meet like-minded people in quality places. No bar scenes or places like that, and don't think that you'll meet someone in the grocery store or in the park. That will not happen for you. Not that you don't have someone waiting—you definitely do.

"It is good that you have realized there was a lesson to be learned in your long period of being alone—it was for you to learn to really appreciate having a mate. In your past lives, you have had a terrible time with your mates. In one life in Indonesia, you were a man who owned a small rice farm. You expected your wife to take care of all the homemaking chores, plus help in the fields. She was a good woman, but you broke her spirit and she died early.

"You must realize that you have overblown expectations so that when your time comes to be with this man, you will balance all aspects of life. You also know that whenever opportunities come your way, you must date for a while. Do not take the first man who crosses your path, for many souls have karma with you and you could have a life with many whose configuration matches yours. So be very clear when you choose the man upcoming. Much love." —**Benclana**

> **Abenda added this note:** "Hi. Lori will be fine in time. She needs to gain some perspective on this situation. Her emotions run deeply and she is taking circumstances personally. She needs to gain control and direct her life."

Anorexic Setback

Q Dear Tara: I am a forty-three year old woman who spent twenty years of my life as an anorexic. In the last few years, however, I have recovered a great deal and no longer feel in danger of sliding back. My problem is that during those years, I retreated from life and from the normal developmental sequence of most adults, i.e., marriage, children, family, friends, social activities. I often despair of ever becoming a real participant in life, although I very much want to. But I have so much fear and embarrassment about my lack of life experience that I feel very shy and inadequate at those times when I do manage to push myself into activities with others in my age group.

Can you and your guides help me understand why I had to go through the experience of anorexia, as well as the feelings I now have about participating in life again? Any information or advice you can give me on this would be appreciated.

S.S.
Santa Barbara, CA

A **A small, dark European woman entered the room to answer Sara's letter:** "We want Sara to be happy, and we are really trying to help her gain some control. She is doing a marvelous job, I might add. You can see that she has had many obstacles to cross. Now all she needs to do is start going to social activities and not be overly sensitive about her previous lack of a life. She has passed many tests and can be proud of herself. She has much to offer others and can help many people who need to work on their self-esteem and phobias. Her example can inspire them, and she can talk to them without realizing how much she is helping them. She needs to realize that life is for living, and that she must hunt for happiness. This means she must make the first move; after that, happiness will follow.

"In her last life, she was the only child of a very rich French family. She was isolated from others because her parents felt that common children weren't good enough for her to play with. She was indulged in food, toys and sweets as a replacement for the companionship of other children. She was a fat, lonely child. When she grew up and was introduced to society, she was rejected for being fat and socially uncultivated. So in this life, she has been thin, but again socially uncultivated. Tell her she doesn't need to be a clown at a party to be noticed. She just needs to be her own sweet self and be open and honest. A smile is all that she needs; that is her social introduction to others. She needs to be the first to smile, then her life will take a tremendous upswing." **—Marie Beaujolais**

Bisexual Seeks Friends

Q Dear Tara: I am writing to ask you for information about a problem I've had my whole life. I know you can't respond to each letter, but I feel many others might suffer from this same problem and could benefit from your advice. My problem is this: I am now thirty years old, during my entire life—childhood as well as adulthood—I have rarely had friends or a mate. I know in my heart that I'm dealing with a karmic lesson. I have explored twenty-two past lives, but have uncovered no specific reason why I have to experience this extreme loneliness.

As a teenager and in early adulthood, I tried to commit suicide several times because of my loneliness, but as I've grown older, I've accepted that this is just a fact of life I have to deal with. I try to look at it as a challenge and not a problem. I don't mean to imply that I've never had a friend or mate, but when I do, it rarely lasts more than four months. My family is very small, just my mother, a great aunt and myself. I have no other living blood relatives. My father left when I was six months old and I've never known him.

Something else that tends to make me feel alienated from most people is the fact that I'm bisexual—not straight and not gay, but bisexual. Although I don't generally openly declare my sexuality to people, I do feel that they perceive me as being strange without quite knowing why.

Basically, I'm a nice guy, down to earth and semi-attractive, so I don't know of a personality or physical flaw that would repel people from me. I have tried everything I can think of to meet friends or a mate—attending classes, asking out co-workers, subliminal tapes on giving and receiving love, counseling, prayer, visualization, channeling, and just being open and friendly. Yet nothing I do seems to help. Please ask Abenda or any of my guides what I can do to lessen the severity of this challenge. Hopefully, other isolated, lonely people can benefit from your advice also.

J.G.
Houston, TX

A **I received this automatic writing from a man named Malcolm:** "Joseph is extremely intelligent and doesn't find a lot of people on his level to converse with. He is really upset that he has no friends, but he will meet people when he reaches out into the right group of people. That time is coming.

"He has had many lives as a monk in Tibet and in medieval Catholic churches, where friendships were not openly allowed. His sexuality also comes from those lives. Although I know I am old-school stuffy, I will try to help him in social situations, since he would like to experience life more openly and fulfillingly. I will tell

you that life is very good for Joseph upcoming. I am glad to be able to write to Joseph through Tara. Thank you."
—Malcolm Breinsworth

Abenda had this to add: "Joseph, you are going to be fine in the near future. You can join a few organizations and meet people at learning seminars. You are not alone in the world. Many people feel that they are alone, but it is only you who holds yourself back. Try not to intellectualize anyone's motives for friendship, as each and every person is self-centered in their actions and intentions, even you.

"Bisexuality is common. All people are made up of androgynous emotions, some women more male, some men more female, some people balanced. Whether people act on their bisexuality is their concern. You are not abnormal, just honest."

Fear of Public Speaking

 Dear Tara: I have worked through many problems in my life, digging out causes and working through to balance, but one persistent problem remains, and this is something I earnestly desire your assistance with.

My problem? Fear of public speaking. All my efforts to overcome it have so far been futile. This problem began when I was a freshman in high school. I should add that this problem is not apparent to others—I am good at speaking and acting and reading poetry, I use my voice well and I can move people, but the terrible, panicky fear has never, ever gone away. Whenever I open my mouth to speak to a group, I can hardly breathe, my heart pounds uncontrollably, and I feel like I'm going to explode. The most ironic thing is that my career choice is to teach Language Arts to eighth-graders. I have no problem with children, only with speaking in front of my peers. It would be such a blessing and a relief to discover something that would give me some clarity and understanding of this situation which has stubbornly remained with me for years.

J.Z.
Van Nuys, CA

A tall, slender woman exquisitely dressed in the style of classical Rome wrote this response: "You rose and spoke in the forums of Rome, you chastised the work of many who did not contribute to the cause of freedom. You were taken from your home and family, kidnapped by strangers in the night, and you found yourself many days' ride in a wilderness, all alone. After a long time, a small group of people found you and took you into their home to live with them. You were very ill and disoriented from your ordeal in the wilderness, and could not remember who you were or where you came from. But you knew how to read and write, so you taught the group learning skills, and this heightened your self-esteem. The news spread and many other people came to live nearby so they and their children could learn to read and write, and have a chance in life.

"This is what you fear; you greatly admire anyone who stands up for their rights, but you have heavy fears that you will lose everything if you protest too loudly about any grievance. You may shake your head and say,

"Well, I live in a cultured society; that would not happen now." But Rome was also a highly cultured society, so subconsciously you are still gripped by this fear. You need only be aware of what you speak, so that you know you will not bring about personal pain. Love and more love." —**Genastia**

> **Note from Abenda:** "What a clear road to get you to be a teacher, but very hard on you in other ways. Develop a more positive outlook. Now that you know the source of your karma, you can alleviate this fear. Start working yourself up a level at a time. Start by speaking to small groups on safe subjects at first, then controversial subjects later, if you so desire."

Closeness Scares Her

Q Dear Tara: I have always been very shy. I was extremely quiet as a child and never talked in class unless the teacher asked me a question. I didn't even talk to the other kids in my class unless they spoke to me first, which rarely happened. I wasn't popular and never had any friends or boyfriends.

As I became an adult, I became a little more talkative, but I'm still shy. I do have a few friends now, but they're more like acquaintances. Whenever I've met people who wanted to be closer to me, I would pull away. Getting close to someone scares me, but I don't know why. I'd like to get close to someone, but I'm scared. I find it impossible to reveal anything personal to someone, though I can talk on and on about other subjects.

I come from a large family and I've never had any problem communicating with them, but I've also never felt close to them either. Can you help me?

Elsa Rodriguez
San Jose, CA

A Abenda introduced me to a friendly, middle-aged woman who wrote this: "During the time of the Black Plague in England, everyone in your family perished but you. You lived on a rambling farm, far from town. When the neighbors died of the plague, you were totally alone. Whenever anyone approached the farm, you hid because you were afraid that they had the plague. You longed for human contact, but at that time, it could have meant death. Even though you suffered tremendous loneliness, you knew that you were lucky to be alive.

"In this life, you feel isolated again, even though you chose a large family to be born into. You can be friends with them. Start by being hospitable and courteous; go out of your way to be helpful. Then start going to organizations and meet others, extend your hand and invite others to go places with you. Do not wait for them—you must take the initiative. Extend your emotions also; no one can hurt you, you only hurt yourself by holding back. You will see a great difference in a short time." —**Lucinda Miles**

Note from Abenda: "You need only to extend your hand and it will be grasped by others. Extend your heart and you will be loved by others. It is better to love and be loved for only a short time than never to have loved or been loved during your lifetime.

81

Trust your intuition about who will be a friend to you.
Open up and experience joy."

A Mundane and Spiritual Impasse

Q Dear Tara: I'm thirty-four years old and still a
virgin, mostly due to fear and mistrust of men
instilled at an early age. Over the years, I've
accepted my life as it is, but recently I feel I've come to
an impasse, both mundane and spiritual. I feel I've spent
my whole life working to achieve distant goals and
always falling short, never coming close. Eventually I
lose interest and give up.

Why is my life like this and will it always be like this?
I know we're here to learn about love and to advance
spiritually, but that's too vague for me. I need some
simple basics. It's hard for me to accept that I purposely
made these choices, and it's getting increasingly harder
to live with them. Please help me to understand.

R.C.S.
Boston, MA

A Abenda and an older woman with a pleas-
ant smile were seated on the couch in our
contact room. The older woman wrote this
answer: "You can overcome your shyness by going to
like-minded events and meetings. You are not really
alone but your fear relates to past-life causes.

"In a past life in Boston during the early 1800s, you
were the daughter of a prostitute. She loved you very
much and sent you away to a nunnery when you were
ten years old so you wouldn't be forced to have the same

life she had. In the convent, you were told many horrible things about your mother and her way of life, but you still loved her very much and knew you were being a good girl to please her. You abided by the dogma and rules of the convent, and in time, you took your vows of celibacy as a nun.

"In this life, you again chose a life in Boston. You have sought the love of your mother through celibacy once again. To break this cycle, you must realize that your mother wanted happiness and security for you. There is nothing wrong with sexuality, she just didn't want your body to be used by many men. That was her desperate attempt to save your reputation among the judgments of that era's society. You can be loved and you can break the cycle. Know that if you need me, I am here for you any time. You have all my love." **—Martha Francis**

> **Note from Abenda:** "You are a product of past programming. If you truly desire to change this, it starts with wisdom. Take it slow, think before you act and have a good time. Life is for living."

Chapter Four

Health

I receive a lot of questions about health from readers. My guides and I have spent much time exploring the concepts of health and its flip-side, disease, and why so many souls incarnating on this plane seem to choose lives that are filled with pain as a way of working out their karma. Let me share a little of their wisdom regarding health and disease.

From Rod Invergordon: "The physical pain in your realm indicates a hard path. You lose much sense of purpose when you lose control of your body, especially when you must be dependent on others.

"Disease is the carry-over of negative karma. The reason you set yourself up to experience disease lies in your karmic past. Soon, people on earth will develop more machines to analyze waves and vibrations; these machines relate back to Atlantis, where sound machines and technology were used for healing. Mankind will then be freed from the limitations of many diseases.

"Be aware that positive karma will result from extending your hands and hearts to help those who cannot help themselves. You can do this in many ways—even a smile carries over to others and can inspire them to be nicer to each other. Have faith and be well."

Abenda wrote the following: "You must realize that those who have pain and ailments are usually brave souls. As an example, they may have decided at an inter-life council meeting to experience cancer and attempt to react positively to their ailments, thus working off guilt and negative karma accumulated from past lives.

"This is a very hard aspect of life; you must help others when you are needed by ailing family or friends. I am referring to the truly sick and needy. You must also know when to stop helping others so they can learn to help themselves. Do not be so full of self-righteousness that you cannot extend a hand to others, as empathy is the way to the Godhead. This earns you wonderful karma. You can practice humanity in many forms, whether you choose to sacrifice in life, love, money, or service. You can make this a joyful or sad experience—it's your choice."

Herpes Problem

Q Dear Tara: You and your guides have helped so many people with a wide variety of problems; I wonder if you could help those of us who have herpes? Some doctors say L-Lysine [an amino acid] is helpful, but it didn't do anything for me. I wonder if there is some karmic or psychological factor that I don't recognize?

E.S.
Portland, OR

A **A tall, distinguished-looking man answered this:** "You should be glad it is not something far worse. You have not given yourself a chance to be stress-free, which has led to disease in your lives upon the earth. In one life, you were a leper and were banished from society. Your confidence in life was that of a mere worm; you did not feel a zest to live. In your last life, in Germany, you got tuberculosis and were put in a sanitarium—again, you were isolated from other people. You died of the tuberculosis, alone and isolated.

"So in this life, you have herpes—maybe as a reminder to protect yourself. Deep down, however, you would like to think all people are good and kind, but on the surface, you are afraid to trust, so you have the herpes. This enables you to keep your distance from others, though it means that you are a very lonely person at times.

"How did all this start? Once you were a very attractive woman in Ireland. Marauders came and hurt you terribly; eventually, they killed you. You think that holding a disease to yourself will protect you from being hurt

87

by others.

"You need to work on learning to trust others so you don't need to hide behind a veil of disease. Know that you are worthy and whole, a spark of the Godhead. You can do it." **—Barbaros Stanzan**

> **Abenda added the following:** "Release your fears. You can have a normal, healthy life and future lives. Medication and vitamins will work, if you let them. Learn to trust yourself first, then learn to trust others. You needn't be afraid any more."

Right-Brain Surgery

Q Dear Tara: I hope and pray that you can help me with this problem. When I was nineteen years old, I underwent surgery on the right side of my brain. Subsequently, I have suffered extreme depression, poverty, and endless random wandering in search of myself.

I feel stuck, like a big boulder is blocking my way out. I feel different from everyone, that I just don't fit. Please help me, I don't know what to do next.

L.A.
Omaha, NE

A **A pleasant-looking red-haired woman who said she was Lynne's guide wrote this response:** "Dear Lynne, you have been given a new life, you must stop reacting in a negative manner. You no longer need to seek the sympathy of others—you are free of that. You can start to enjoy life. Look around you and change your attitude. When you do, a multitude

of love and happiness will completely enfold you." —
Patricia

> **Note from Abenda:** "You need to realize that all
> things, both negative and positive, work for a reason.
> You had surgery to help you overcome a karmic
> problem. Are you going to continue in a positive or
> negative way? Only you can decide, but life is waiting
> for you."

Night Problem

Q Dear Tara: I'm writing to you for help with a
problem I've had since childhood. For some
reason, I feel that this has something to do with
my past, but I don't know what it could have been. The
problem is physical. It usually starts at night—I'll be fine,
then a second later, I'll get hot flashes followed by
nausea. I'll start crying and shaking. I did see a doctor,
who prescribed nerve pills, which I have been taking for
the last ten years. What could have happened to me to
cause such a problem since childhood? My family feels
I should just pray and leave it in God's hands. I have done
this for many years. Could you and Abenda please try
and help me find out the cause and the cure for this—it
is controlling my life.
                                                        L.H.
                                          Minneapolis, MN

A **Automatic writing received:** "In many past
lives, Linda was a coal miner; in others she was
a cave dweller. The problems she is having
relate to feelings of claustrophobia, which are a carry-

over from these lives. She has a nervous temperament—her body flushes from nervous reactions and she feels she cannot hold her food. She needs to start doing yoga and deep breathing. She doesn't need to worry about her life; all will be well." **—In love, Manieaka**

> **Note from Abenda:** "You are a part of God, and as such, you are holy—you do not have to be holy in a church to be holy. Release the effect of this cause, take control of your life. Pray, but pray the way you want to pray. As part of your prayers or meditations, include a mantra and chant, 'I now know the cause of my night responses, and I release the effect.' Repeat it over and over as you visualize yourself free of the nervous reactions."

Partially Blind and Deaf

Q Dear Tara: I hope you and your guides can help me with this problem. What did I do or what am I now doing that has caused me to go blind in my right eye and deaf in my left ear? I also suffer daily headaches and lack of energy and vitality. How can I reverse these conditions? The blindness was diagnosed as closed-angle glaucoma and the deafness was diagnosed as nerve damage. Many thanks and God bless you.

M.S.
Silver Spring, MD

A **Abenda responded first:** "You must try to rely on your guide to help you through this physical crisis. You feel pain so deeply on the gravity plane. You must have dual action as well as acceptance.

Fight in positive ways. It is time to heal."

A sweet-faced older woman wrote this: "You need to relax and not be so hard on yourself. You feel that you have failed to help those less fortunate in past lives, so you chose to be born normal in this lifetime and then experience handicaps yourself. But now that these circumstances have come to pass, you are panicked.

"You must realize fully, on every level, that you are a good and worthwhile person. You must heal your inner self as well as your outer self. You can accomplish this through many changes. First, you must open yourself to the light. Visualize your head being surrounded in pale blue and green light; this will help heal the headaches and loss of sight and hearing. Learn to eat more healthfully; proper nutrition will help on a deep cellular level. You are worrying too much; learn to relax more. Use deep breathing for panic attacks. When you feel afraid, call on me and I will be there to help you. I am your guide and am with you always." **—Renee Fran**

Bulimia Problem

Dear Tara: As much as I try, I cannot seem to rid myself of an eating disorder, bulimia, which has plagued me most of my adult life. I generally begin the cycle with feelings of panic and emptiness. I visualize the need for food as though it is the last meal I will ever have. I have a compulsive urge to steal food, then I secretly gorge myself. Afterward, I induce vomiting. This is always followed by severe self-recrimination and feelings of worthlessness. I then resolve to never do it again, but invariably, the cycle repeats itself.

I have done some past-life explorations and know that I have had lifetimes of famine and poverty. I have also experienced lifetimes of obesity, excess and self-indulgence. It is my guess that these influences have converged to form dual fears: one of starvation, the other of obesity.

Could you please help shed some light on the "why's" of this behavior and give me a hint on how to quit? I've tried numerous self-help books and have briefly attended a twelve-step program, with virtually no success.

R.M.
Denver, CO

An older woman with an English accent stepped in to answer Reyna: "First, you must stop the shoplifting. Go grocery shopping and pay for the food you will eat. On a Sunday or on a day off, make enough casseroles and main course dishes for the following week. Package them in portions and fill up your freezer. Whenever you open your freezer, you can see that there is enough food there for you, that you will not starve. Each day, thaw enough food for that day, and when you eat, eat slowly.

"Bulimia is a bad habit. Since you have been doing it for so many years, your body has expectations and your guilt drives you to do it. You can overcome this. You need to find a support group in your area; this will help you with your feelings of secrecy, guilt and inadequacy. Many people suffer from this problem. In addition, seek advice and counseling from a professional. This can usually be found at very low cost. Professionals have been trained in techniques and information which cannot be found in support groups, books or tapes, no matter how good.

"You are correct in your perception of your past lives. In particular, in one life, you were a beggar and could never get enough to eat, so you stole food in the market square to get by. You were scorned and shunned by the townspeople. In the very next lifetime, you were born into a stable, middle-class family who thought love was expressed with food. They fed you until you were such a rotund little beast that you could hardly even move your limbs. So in this lifetime, you find yourself emotionally alternating between the lessons of both lifetimes.

"You need to release the effects of those lives. You can start to do this by developing your talents. Also, learn to be less preoccupied with thoughts of yourself and your inner workings. Reach out to others; they can help you break your self-absorption. This will lead you down the path of self-knowledge and inner worth in a way you never dreamed possible.

"In my last lifetime, I was a teacher and counselor at a private all-girls school in England, so I understand what you are going through. I have seen this many times in young girls. But you can overcome it and learn to live a beautiful, satisfying life." **—Elizabeth "Betsy" Worthfield**

> **Abenda added the following:** "All will go well for you. Trust your inner convictions to better your life. Sometimes guilt and shame can drive you to seek moral escape, or it can cause you to succeed and achieve. You are at this crossroads of deciding which you will do, but you must not *try*, you simply must *do it*, as 'trying' is a lie. Take baby steps in the right direction. When you are afraid, ask Betsy to help you conquer this."

Ashram Disaster

 Dear Tara: I have been following your "Cause and Effect" column for some time now. It has given me hope that I might find an answer to my husband's problems.

Twenty years ago, he entered an ashram in Malibu, where he endured an eleven-month-long training with a severe teacher. He was taught to use a certain type of breathing, along with yoga postures and month-long fasts. Then my husband experienced a severe psychic opening. He was not told what was happening and was greatly afraid. He was close to death, weighing only ninety-eight pounds at six foot two, and battling with the most horrible images psychically. Ever since that time, he has had no control over his imagination. He has sought healing from many spiritual teachers, psychics and therapists. Needless to say, this has been a severe strain on our marriage, as he is extremely paranoid. He has had to give up teaching, being in crowds or anywhere near other people. Our social life is zero and our sex life is not much better, as he is even paranoid of me at times.

I would love to see him be happy and normal again, as he is such a sweet person when he's not afraid.

M.H.
Seattle, WA

A **A handsome, middle-aged man appeared and said he had known your husband in a past life. He had this to say:** "In the 15th Century, your husband was a Catholic priest who forced others to flog themselves for all ungodly thoughts. He was so strict and moral that he was highly amoral. Myra didn't experience that lifetime with him. This life, he needed to learn firsthand the repercussions of this kind of severity. Another incarnation relating to his current problem was in 1690 as a woodsman who trapped and sold furs in Romania. He never wanted people around. He thought of them as greedy and selfish, and they were to him in response to his rigidity. In this life, he strived so hard for purity that he lost his stability. Myra will help him regain what was lost, for she was once an Indian Shaman visionary. She does not openly practice this today, but she retains the ability to help others find peace." **—Brien Frie**

Abenda added this: "Part of the problem stems from the massive weight loss he endured in the ashram. This created a chemical imbalance, which contributes to spaciness and loss of touch with reality. If he has not had a proper diet since—plenty of protein, amino acids, vitamins and minerals—these nutrients and muscle tissue have not been replenished. Seek out a professional to guide you. A nutritionist can help you regulate his diet, which will help ground him and correct the problem."

Weight Loss Block?

Q Dear Tara: I have been working hard on overcoming my weight problem, but I think there may be a block that is keeping me from attaining my goal. I feel that through automatic writing, you may find some new insights about this block. When I tried to participate in an experimental program on weight loss, I felt resentful and angry, and got nowhere.

I have some ideas of why I am overweight. I grew up in a dysfunctional family—my mom was mentally ill and in a hospital for many years. My dad had to work all the time to support me and my three sisters. This was during the '60s, when mental illness was a taboo subject. My sisters and I had no one to talk to about our fears. I learned to cope with my fears by eating. Naturally, I gained weight. I overcame that and discovered that I got a lot of attention from men. At first I liked this, but then I realized that the attention I was getting was for my appearance, my shell, not the real me. During this time, I married, and later had a beautiful daughter. Like a lot of women, I gained weight during my pregnancy. Unlike a lot of women, I didn't lose it after the baby was born. I faced a lot of challenges during that period of my life and found that food acted as a buffer against unwanted feelings.

For the past several years, I have been trying to learn to re-direct the energy I feel when I am faced with a difficult moment and feel compelled to eat. I do try to eat healthfully—no caffeine, no sugar, no salt, but I still crave food, especially carbohydrates.

For the most part I am very happy with my life. I have overcome the sense of not being accepted by others by reaching out to others first. I know that people are attracted to me naturally, as I am a happy, outgoing person. I am an integral part of the school system and community through my volunteer work, I have expanded my art career, I teach crafts, and my design ideas are well-received by manufacturers and magazines.

Despite this, I still feel that there is a block keeping me from dealing with my weight, that there is some hidden fear and I use my weight to protect me.

L.C.
Sharon, WI

A beautiful young girl showed up to answer Leslie's letter: "You stumble around in this life as though you didn't choose the circumstances, but you did. Although you think that you are burdened by circumstances, they make you grow. You are learning, aren't you? Why you feel you need to deal with these events and milestones in your life is because you don't feel you truly deserve love. As a child, your mother was away, and you felt abandoned. Food was a natural source for your security. Now you are trying to take away your security, and find yourself resentful and angry over losing your food intake.

"In a past life, you were a beautiful young girl in Malaysia. You were determined to go into the city and make a name for yourself. So you did just that, and became a singer in the dens. Many men were in love with you, and you had a child. That child was shuffled from one lounge to another. You finally suffered a nervous breakdown due to exhaustion and drugs, and acted crazy until some people came and took you away. Your daughter was left behind, lost and forlorn. She had no sense of security and became a prostitute, looking for someone to take care of her. After a few years, when you were rested and restored, you found her but she would have nothing to do with you. You felt terrible that you had let your daughter down. In this life, you wanted to experience the abandonment that your daughter had experienced in the previous lifetime.

"In another lifetime, you were a poor beggar girl in Indonesia. You had no friends or family to help you except the other beggar children. You were always hungry and insecure. You died very young in that lifetime.

"You have carried the security issue with you into this lifetime. In time, you will let go of the negative effects and know that you are worthy of a nice body as well as a good life." —**Rosinta Thilio**

Keeping Husband Awake

Q Dear Tara: I have a problem I have never seen addressed in any advice column I have read. I hope you can ask your guides to help me with this one. Since I was a little girl, I have talked in my sleep. Sometimes I scream and wake up the entire household. I always feel fine when I wake up and never remember any bad dreams, but my husband is complaining. He doesn't get much sleep because I wake him up three or four times a night with my talking and screaming. He says I can make myself stop subconsciously, but I've tried and it hasn't worked so far. Is there anyway I can learn to stop talking and screaming in my sleep so my husband can get his rest at night?

M.O.
San Diego, CA

 Michelle's guide appeared, a tall, slender woman named Amanda. She wrote this: "Michelle is talking to me and to others as she sleeps. She has many friends here. She should record herself using a voice-activated recorder. She should also keep a journal of her communications.

"Regarding her screaming: While she is asleep, she is like a little girl who doesn't realize she is talking loudly. She is not afraid, that is why she feels fine and doesn't remember any nightmares when she wakes up because there aren't any. She is just communicating too loudly with those of us on the other side. Her husband would be less angry if he wore ear plugs until Michelle can learn to control her nightly communications. She can do this by learning self-hypnosis. Then she can talk to us during waking hours instead of at night when her husband is trying to sleep." **—Amanda**

Mental Illness

Q Dear Tara: Can you please give me some insight on how to get the mentally ill to respond to responsibility? Nothing seems to work. Why is it that you can't reach some people? I have been mentally ill myself, but I am a lot better off now. I want to help others who are mentally ill to overcome their feeling of pain and emptiness.

K.R.
Malone, NY

A **Abenda introduced a woman Martha, who wrote this:** "Kevin, we know that life has tossed you a few curve balls, but you seem to be steadying your nerves and feeling more comfortable on the earth plane and in your body. You are overcoming your tests very well. You cannot recall how you wound up this way, but it stems from past lifetimes. In one life, you were an African who was captured by a rival tribe and tortured to death for poaching on their hunting ground. In another life in medieval England, you were tortured and killed for robbing people.

"You no longer feel that you have to torture yourself, so you are well on the road to healing. As for others, they need to experience their soul journey and their pain. They cannot tell you the reasons for their turmoil because they have not completely worked through it. But it is good that you are beginning to want to help others overcome life's troubles and destructive patterns. You will be a good counselor, as you know what it is like to suffer mental pain and turmoil, and you can guide them through their pain. Good luck to you; I will be here to guide you." **—Martha Schmidt**

> **Note from Abenda:** "This will be good for Kevin. Martha and Kevin have known each other through many lifetimes; in some they were comrades and were shot and tortured together. Martha broke out of that karmic configuration and studied psychiatry for many years. She is a guide who has recently been assigned to Kevin to help him on his continued path toward enlightenment. She will help him learn to channel his newfound insight and direction to help others."

After Vietnam

Q Dear Tara: I've spent many years and a lot of money running around to psychics, channelers, astrologers, etc., as well as books and tapes, but I still cannot find the reason for the last fifteen years of pain and limitation. So please, Tara, would you help me find out why?

I was a happy and healthy young man when I went to Vietnam at the age of eighteen. When I got out, I was a little messed up, wild and crazy, but still healthy. Then, at age twenty-seven, my muscular two-hundred-pound body dropped seventy pounds. I experienced sweating and pain, and my joints were "mysteriously" deteriorating. Doctors said it was some kind of unusual arthritis, but I have always wondered whether I was exposed to chemicals when I was in Vietnam, such as Agent Orange or some other top-secret chemical.

I worked through some of the anger I felt and became confident that I could cure myself through holistic medicine. I did enough stuff to cure five diseases, but still I got worse. Eventually, about the time I started to think in terms of ending the pain with a bullet in the brain, a book came to me about reincarnation, karma and why we choose the things we do to learn from. That was when I realized there was more to this than simply being poisoned by chemicals.

I've read about people who explored their past lives, discovering how those past lives created diseases they had in this life, and how this knowledge made the disease easier to handle. It would help me a great deal to know where my disease came from and why I created all this pain and suffering in this lifetime.

Although I'm on a good spiritual path now and understand so much more, there are times when I get tired of the struggle, the pain, limitation, drugs and surgeries. It's wearing me out and I'm looking forward to peace on the other side. But before I leave this life, I'd like to know if I've learned what I'm supposed to learn from this disease?

R.W.
Williamsburg, NM

 A handsome young man and a young woman with dark hair and dark eyes were seated comfortably on the couch. The young man

reached eagerly for the notepad to answer: "Yes, yes, yes. We got sprayed in 'Nam. I don't know why, they didn't tell us. They didn't need to do that to anyone, they knew it was deadly stuff. They were just selfish and didn't care what happened to us boys. When I got home from 'Nam, I was twenty-two. None of us knew we had been sprayed with deadly chemicals in 'Nam, so when I got sick and the doctors couldn't figure out what was wrong with me, they told me I was a hypochondriac. I died from complications of a rare lung pneumonia at the age of twenty-seven. I have been a warrior in many lifetimes, the most recent before this last one was in Nazi Germany during World War II. I came back too quick and I'm tired of dying in wars. I won't come back for sometime because I want to live a longer, more productive life next time. Well, Aleethia is waiting to talk to Rick; I just wanted him to know he's not alone." **—Ray Howard**

The dark-haired young woman took the pad then wrote this: "My, I've wanted to talk to you for sometime about this situation, Rick. You have only to open the channel of communication and I will talk to you via writing or speaking in meditation. You were exposed to several chemicals, some directly, some indirectly. Many people have worked hard to cover the scandal.

"You must be brave and carry on. Your work is not finished yet. You are to give hope and inspiration to many; that is your dharma, your direction of service. You have been through so much, but you need to help others try to attain peace of mind while they are still on the earth plane. It is a gift that you have; others listen to you and are attracted to your light. Keep smiling and know that you are a healer, a healer in most senses. You are going through a slower period than before, but life is picking up. You need to express the real you. You have had many lifetimes in which you abused power and privilege.

"We are sorry that you must endure physical pain, but you can keep meditating it away. Don't hold onto your discomforts and pain—let them fly free. Read some herbalogy books; use herbs and vitamins to help maintain strength and vigor. You will be fine; entertain only thoughts of love, which will in turn be attracted to you. Know that greater good comes out of all experience and do not despair. Fly free; don't let others stop you."
—Aleethia Benego

A Stroke and Parkinson's Disease

 Dear Tara: My husband had a stroke when he was only forty-three years old, leaving him handicapped on his entire left side. He is sixty now, and two years ago was diagnosed as having Parkinson's Disease. This is also a disabling disease which is progressing rapidly. Is all this karma? Is there anything we can do? Also, please send our love to all the members of our families who have passed on. Thank you.

H.J.
Ashland, OR

 Abenda brought two women who wanted to respond to Helga's letter. The first said she had lived in Eastern Europe with Helga

in a past life: "You have been kind and good to others in this life. Your dharma has been fulfilled much in this life by your caring for others. You will gain many rewards on earth in future lives as goodness and light and the breath of life continues throughout the ages for the followers who seek it. I hope that you will know that I reach out to help you through the tough moments of life. You are loved." **—Kellimina Forkunz**

From the second woman: "Her husband was away on a ship when she became ill with bubonic plague. When he returned home, he nursed her the best he could, even though he got the plague from her and died a while after she died. She still carries guilt for bringing the plague home to her husband and child. She never forgot his kindness for helping her and the child try to come to grips with those final weeks. Now she gains much from helping others and would never turn away from her husband in this life. He can now transcend a pattern of becoming sick so that you stay in his life. He also needs to release his guilt." **—Harriett Wass**

> **Abenda added this note:** "You know that on this side, when one crosses, it is a great honor to have helped others on the earth plane to overcome their pain and sadness. In the future, you will be able to relax and find the magic in all creation. Much love to you."

Suffers Severe Migraine Headaches

Dear Tara: I am experiencing a karmic event that I cannot seem to clear up by myself. I have used meditation, healing acceleration and many of your tapes, but have continued to suffer, for eight years now, severe vascular migraine headaches every day. The more I try to understand it, the deeper the problem gets.

I have had CAT-scans, EEGs, thyroid testing as well as eighteen injections into the occipital region of my head. Though they weren't able to discover any "physical" defect, they decided to treat me with massive drug therapy.

Finally, after eight years of this nightmare, I went through drug withdrawal by myself and have been using an electrical unit to work out the trigger points at the back of my head and shoulders. I still get migraines, but only about once a week, which is a vast improvement.

I need an answer for the reason I chose to experience this kind of pain in this lifetime. I've been dragging something around for too long, but I've blocked what that something is. The problem can only be solved by looking at it squarely. I would greatly appreciate your help in uncovering the reason I chose this experience.

N.C.
Zumbrota, MN

Abenda introduced me to an elderly gentleman with a kind smile. He wrote this response: "You have allergies that are affecting your blood chemistry. This causes you to react with severe headaches. This is karma from your last lifetime when you helped put many prisoners into Nazi concentration camps. You felt much grief for these poor helpless people because your sense of honor was against it, but you also felt you couldn't disobey orders.

"This time, you hope you have run away from this pain, but it is still in your head. You need to let it go. It would help you to eat well and try not to get stressed as this triggers your subconscious. You are to forgive yourself, for you did empathize with the prisoners and you knew that what was happening was wrong. This knowledge is the key to unlock those pent-up feelings." — **Nolan Yarbrough**

> **Abenda added this note:** "You must release your tendency to hold on to the past. You are a beacon of light to both the meek and the mighty. Relax, study, and know that karma needs to be recognized. You cannot save all people from their pain; our karma is our own."

Agoraphobia

 Dear Tara: When my parents divorced in my teen years, my father, an overly serious, stern workaholic, won custody of all five of us kids. Three months after the divorce, he married his girlfriend and she moved in. One night at the dinner table, my father asked how we were making the adjustments and if anyone wanted to talk about it? I related my feelings and my stepmother began to cry. My father was furious and ordered me to apologize. I was in such pain. From that moment on, I started to repress my feelings and become a "people pleaser." I'd do anything to keep the peace.

When I turned eighteen, I left home and after a series of incidents I realized I was agoraphobic. I'm twenty-five now and it's a little better. I can travel freely in and around a one-hour radius of my house with no trouble. But even a day trip two hours away requires a lot of psyching up and at times a mild tranquilizer.

I am happily married and my husband has been very patient with me. He's a Sagittarius and loves to travel.

Why do I have this karma?

**Shiawann
Royal Oak, MI**

 A young girl was present to answer Shiawann's request. This is what she wrote: "Dear Shiawann, the reason you cannot go places is because you left your children by a river when you were washing clothes in India, and your second child, a son of four years, drowned. You felt that if you had stayed within the realm of your village this wouldn't have happened.

"In another life, as an Irish immigrant in New York, you allowed yourself to drown in a river as a karmic balance for your guilt. So the guilt from the Indian lifetime should already be alleviated. You need to forgive yourself. You have much to offer others, and it is time to let go of this effect. You will experience a peaceful, wholesome life this time. You must do fun and challenging things. Keep taking small trips and work your way up to larger ones. You will always prefer your home, but do not let this stop you from enjoying life." **—Yan-cashka**

> **Abenda added:** "Shiawann is going to be fine in time, now that she knows the source of her fear. When you meditate, do hypnosis or say your prayers, include a statement to the effect of, 'I know the cause of the agoraphobia, and I now release the effect. I travel freely and relaxed, always enjoying my journeys.' Say it over and over many times like a mantra, and visualize yourself traveling with your husband to the places of your dreams."

Third Open-Heart Surgery

Q Dear Tara: My life is full of love, happiness and balance, and I am in tune with myself, God and the world. But I have a very rare disease that now requires me to have a third open-heart surgery to remove a tumor. I know tumors represent a loss of someone or something, but I really feel that I have forgiven others and dealt with the past. I listen to myself, do dream analysis and meditation, but I still can't find a clue as to why this has been going on so long.

B.R.
Bellmore, NY

A **Abenda introduced a woman named Marcellia who said she knew Barbara. The woman was dressed in a flowing, old-fashioned white dress and wore a hat. This is what she wrote:** "Barbara is so lovely. This problem is because of the royal blood in her last life and especially the warrior lineage of many lifetimes. She was a hemophiliac. It was very hard on her, but she was most brave, as she will continue to be this time. She must let go of this affliction; it's the result of guilt for being a warrior in so many lives. She wants out of that, just as she did last life as a boy with hemophilia, which insured his uselessness as a warrior.

"This time Barbara came in as a woman, hoping her gender would protect her, but this heart and blood trouble carried over. Barbara must continue to promote her peaceful, loving side. Maybe she's frustrated by not getting ahead, but she needs to know she can do anything peacefully." —**Marcellia**

Weight Problem From Past Life

Q Dear Tara: About fifteen years ago, I was addicted to amphetamines and was able to keep my weight down to 130 pounds. I looked great but suffered terrible side effects from the drug, which I finally kicked. Somehow, I managed to maintain my weight within a few pounds for about a year, even after having my first son. I am short—five foot three inches—with a medium frame; now I weigh 153 pounds. I've spent a fortune on every diet, every diet book and every diet tape I can lay my hands on. I do advanced aerobic dancing three to four times a week, and I walk a lot. I've gone to a nutritionist and take a very good multi-vitamin and mineral supplement.

I pray for the knowledge and the strength to heal this problem. My husband is happy with me, but I'm not. I really don't feel happy or comfortable with myself at this weight. Please, if you have any insight into my weight problem, let me know.

D.B.
Croton, NY

A **woman named Hilda showed up and said she loved Doreen and wanted to talk to her. This is what she wrote:** "In Rome, Doreen would not share her rations with other hungry people who she knew needed her assistance. She was just being sparing and thinking ahead, but she felt a lot of guilt associated with these very hungry people. This started a chain reaction throughout many lifetimes in which Doreen wanted for food or starved to death.

"More recently, during a lifetime in Italy in 1904, she was a child living on the street. She was kicked about like a dog, and died in the gutter, no consequence to anyone. So now she feels that to eat is to give a body strength and vitality. She doesn't realize she can safely cut back. She must be careful not to overfeed her children. She is so worried about food. She must relax and realize she is in America and will always have food and a good life." **—Hilda**

> **Abenda added this note:** "To relieve her subconscious guilt, which has created the problem, Doreen can donate food, money or time to a homeless shelter. She must stop feeling guilty. It will also serve her to gain self-confidence and then relax. She will be liked, no matter what her weight. She doesn't need to worry about it."

Note from Tara: When this response ran in my

column in *Master of Life WINNERS,* Doreen responded by writing to say that she had experienced this exact Italian lifetime in a 1988 past-life regression. She added that her father, "who is not a generous man," contributes money regularly to an Italian children's charity. She says he always tells her, "You've never seen starvation until you see how it is with the street children in Italy."

Chapter Five

Life Direction

As we go through life, at one time or another, most of us ask the same questions: Who am I? Why am I here? What is my purpose in life? My truth is, you are a spiritual being committed to growth. By incarnating upon the earth, you experience opportunities to learn what works and what doesn't. When you make mistakes, you are given a chance to correct them before trying again—to test yourself until you get it right. Your past experiences have created the character to fulfill your dharma, your service work, which is your life direction.

I'll now let Abenda and Rod Invergordon share what they had to say on the subject.

Abenda wrote this: "Your dharma is your career; we all have it, even those of us on this side. My purpose is to guide Tara. This seems like it would be an easy job as I am dead and most of you think I should laze around and relax after lives, but I am trying to evolve to. We all strive to evolve, and as Tara fulfills her purpose, I fulfill mine. Here I have more clarity, I know more about how life and the universe work, and I can see the past—Tara's past lives, plus her future potentials. So I am comfortable helping Tara and now, through Tara, communicating with you. For me, money, power and prestige are of no consequence, but if I can help you attain goodness, it is a huge consequence for me.

"I must say that both Tara and I knew of these choices that she would make in her life. She has been prepared for this life with many incarnations, and at times it has not been easy for her. She was directed into metaphysics and pushed into automatic writing, but I made it fun for her and answered many of her questions. She had no idea she would help the tribe to communicate. The tribe consists of many souls who are dedicated to help others help themselves, mainly through a mix of Eastern/Western philosophy and the general seeking of goodness in life. Tara is becoming comfortable with her dharma, but before this, she had no idea on a conscious level. Many of you may have no idea what your purpose is. To find out, you must channel the light, seek your positive, good qualities within your personality and your talents. This is a gift, and you are to use your gifts."

"The soul will continue on, whether or not you seek a religious base in your earthly life. What is important is the condition of your karma when you die. Not all people are destined for spiritual healing or to seek spirituality. Everyone finds it in their own time and in their own way. You are always to treat yourself and others with love and respect; this is a pure form of Godliness. You are not to judge others, or hate others who do not believe as you do. You are to be a channel for the light and a guide for peace. Send light and love to all."

From Rod Invergordon: "Some have dharma that they must fulfill on a certain path. An example is your husband Richard's dharma to communicate metaphysical principles. Power and leadership can be the life direction of some, but how you handle the power is up to your sense of righteousness and judgment. Sometimes money comes with this package, sometimes not. Prestige, whether it be community or global, claims power. More people are apt to follow a successful person. With power and leadership comes the passion of ideas, and this stirs envy in men. So only the very bold create followers.

"Spirituality is a way of discovering the secrets of the universe. As mankind discovers more and more about the universe, his science is beginning to draw closer and closer to spirituality. Eventually, the two will become one. However, as you are still on the earth plane, it is safest to maintain a middle-of-the-road attitude about all matters pertaining to spirituality. This is because what is so simple seems so complex and jumbled to human minds. You must progress further down the road before you truly begin to understand.

"Religions are neither right nor wrong. Some people must belong to a community. The sin they commit is in assuming that all people want to belong to a community. Help each other in an unconditional way; do not try and convert others to what you think is the true God or true path of life; everyone has their own way of seeing the glory of God."

Looking For Life Goals

Q Dear Tara: I am completely frustrated at the moment and don't know where else to turn. I know how busy you are, Tara, but I'm at my wit's end and hope you can help me.

Please ask Abenda why am I still having difficulty doing what it is that I am supposed to do and am I doing it correctly?

I'm almost fifty years old, and I'm not sure what I'm supposed to accomplish in this lifetime. I'm so confused, I feel like I have lived my whole life in a fog. Can you help?

**J.W.
Memphis, TN**

A **Abenda and I stood in our contact house and watched two men stroll through the garden toward the front door. They entered, introduced themselves and said they wished to help JoAnne. The first man had this to say:** "You are going through times when it is slow for most people of your society. The structure is swaying, and you feel like you are drowning within the system.

"You are not alone, but you must not dwell on the negatives in life but on the positives. You have many positive aspects in your life, and you do not think of them as such. You need to gain some new skills and training. You can get ahead, and you can if you apply yourself. So take heart and remember that life is what we make of it. It is either a tranquil oneness or a harsh separateness. It is all in how you view life. You can have all that you want in time." **—Frank Wells**

The other man picked up the pen and wrote: "JoAnne, you are a bright woman and you can start your life anew by practicing your bright ideas with others. You need to reach out and touch others with your knowledge and wisdom. You know what you know and who you are; your next step is to grow into those mature shoes and take yourself seriously and respectfully."—**Tom Sands**

Abenda added this note: "You are not to fear life's downtrodden moments as this is part of the life cycle and your own individual karma. You are to remember the good of life and grasp it. Hold onto it and expect that good things should be yours."

He Doesn't Want to Be Black

Q Dear Tara: I remember when I was very young, I had a hard time accepting the fact that I was black. For a long time I constantly wished to be white. After a while, sometimes I would actually think that I was white, because I'm very light-skinned. Eventually, as I grew up, I accepted my situation, but even to this day, I have a strong affinity with white people and a slight aversion toward black people or other races.

Could this possibly stem from past lives? I would be extremely grateful if you could give me some insight to my problem.

D.L.
Westchester, NY

 There was quite a crowd waiting to respond to Dave's letter. The first was a big, extroverted black woman who wore very color-

ful clothes and a turquoise, white, pink and yellow turban on her head. She wrote first: "In many past lives, Dave persecuted the black man, not horrifically, but through exploitation. Now he must face being a black person and the prejudices this world still has to work through. Dave is very intelligent but he cannot get ahead as well as he could because of his color. He must learn to release this karmic effect and work toward becoming of positive service. He will come into his own if he decides to go forth and really try. He must learn to have compassion, even for the American Indian and other nationalities. This is meant for him to learn in this life; as he learns it, his life will become better and better. I also want to say that he is to be cheerful and love himself for his color; this will be a steppingstone in the right direction. Be joyful, Dave." **—Bettina**

Abenda added this brief note: "Dave needs to love himself unconditionally. He is such a special person, he can do anything he sets his mind to do. He needs to relax and trust in his abilities."

An older black man was the next to write: "Dave gave orders for men to beat us and scare us into working for him, because we would have left and gone back to our villages. It is most interesting that he is black in this lifetime as he is now in the same introverted position as I was in that lifetime. You must make the best of your situation. I did. I had many friends and later died a contented old man." **—Fhami Swah**

An man in a white colonial suit was the last to communicate: "Dave also had a good life in China as an herbal healer. He was loved by many people because he really tried. He should not forget where he came from. He will now realize he has power and gifts to give others, and he will start going forward in a very positive channel." **—Henri Lac**

Psychic Ability

 Dear Tara: Ever since I was a child, I knew I was "different" in the sense that I was in touch with different planes. I knew things that were going to happen—usually deaths in the family before they happened—even if I'd never seen the person involved. I subdued my abilities for many years because I felt unable to control the situation and the negative reactions from family and friends.

Now that I know more and want to help people with my knowledge, I find I'm blocked. I'm not able to go into deep meditation, or concentrate long enough to contact my guides, or do any of the things I know I have the ability to do. I don't know what to do to start things flowing again. Even my visualization ability is fuzzy and elusive. I feel frustrated. Can you help me?

J.H.
Portland, OR

 Abenda called two of Joann's guides in to answer her question. The first one was a dark-haired young Gypsy girl, who wrote: "Some are to open channels, some are to close the channels. Practice makes perfect. But you are never to be tactless and predict a negative future event. That is not positive for channels, which is why there are not that many true channels. But, of course, we all have psychic meanings and symbols and tools to use. The best thing I can advise is to continue meditating, asking to reopen the channels, but don't try to force it. Relax. Let it happen. Practice your craft. It takes time and much patience. Keep journals, monitor your dreams." **—Willamina**

Abenda added this note: "Willamina is right— not everyone is psychic, but those who are can develop it with a conscious conscience. You need to trust yourself and take some training and read books. The advice Willamina gave you about keeping journals and diaries is very sound. By recording your dreams, thoughts and actual day-to-day experiences, you can see how they correlate. I'll have Yong-Pen write about Joann's blockages."

A tiny Oriental man who wore a monk's robes wrote the following: "Joann has lived many lives as a monk in Tibet. She has this ancient knowledge, but sometimes doesn't feel holy enough to use the powers. Even though she isn't in a monastery this time, she should understand that she can still use this power. This is why it is so important for her to release her blocks. She will get much out of all her experiences." **—Yong-Pen**

Karmic Accidents?

 Dear Tara: Several months ago I was reading a book dealing with metaphysics. Although I agreed with most of what it said relating to karma, it also said something I had never heard before. It said that even though we plan most of our main goals and direction between lives, sometimes, once we get in the physical plane, accidents occur. For example, you plan to live to a ripe old age and accomplish numerous things but something outside yourself interferes and your life is cut short; you didn't "mean it to happen." How can this be?

At the time I read this, my mind automatically went to my father, who died in an auto accident when I was thirteen. Besides the natural feelings of losing a parent, feeling as if this shouldn't have happened, I keep wondering if it possibly could have been a karmic accident? If so, what happened for him next?

Please ask Abenda and your guides to comment on this for me, and thank them for me.

P.M.
Old Saybrook, CT

 A slender man of medium height with short hair sat on the couch next to Abenda. He accepted the notepad and pen and began to write: "It is of great consequences that you and everyone else of your realm pick out what they want to accomplish in the life before they are born. This is done at the council, which is not exactly like going over a list of details with a life-instruction counselor. It happens at a very fast rate through vibrational tones in a spiral of energy.

"It is possible for you to resist and even reverse some of your choices. Your father, like many others, are just fulfilling their karma so they can rise higher on the vibrational chain to become one with the godhead. Your dad misses having been there for you. Even though a person may have chosen the circumstances on the other side, they are not always prepared to cross the barrier, so you can see why some people get upset when they cross and feel like it was an accident. Their conscious mind is not in synch with their unconscious motivations and circumstances of their lives.

"There are no accidents. To make the break out of your earthly shell usually takes weeks of preparation, sometimes months, which is why it is possible to change circumstances with wisdom. You prepare your soul to make the transition from the body, which is why so many psychics and sensitives can pick up or see the transition phase or 'accident' that may be coming. The preparation process can even start years in advance, in some cases. It is possible to see the life path through astrology and palmistry as well. Still, you would have to be on top of any specific destined situation you want to change, months or years in advance, in order to change it. This does happen; changes are clearly seen through life in everyday society." **—Mike Olson**

Abenda smiled approvingly at Mike and took the pen to communicate this: "I think Mike was right on target and has explained the process of earthly accidents to you. He could have added that it's resistance to any kind of suffering that really scares humankind. You feel like maybe you could alleviate the pain and suffering of a horrible accident, but I have tried to stress this to Tara many times: When your time is up, it's up. No use fighting your predestined circumstances. It is a transition of your life and soul. It is okay to be here on this side of existence. I have both loved and dreaded earthly lives, but I have learned, and that is the importance of the earthly phase.

"Patricia, you should be happy for having known and loved your father, even though it was only for a short while. You were born to be together and you will meet again and again, if you so desire."

A Shield of Distrust

Q Dear Tara: About seven years ago, when I was thirty-five, I tried to break away from my mother's unhealthy need to mother me and my unhealthy need to be mothered. As a result, there has grown a great distance between us.

Also, about three years ago, a relationship with someone I loved ended. I can still feel the devastation that gripped me. There was no closure on the relationship at the end. Now I have a shield of cold distrust surrounding me and I feel completely unable to love. It seems to me that human behavior is the result of selfish motives or guilt coming from a basis of fear. I have tried but cannot seem to transcend whatever is blocking me. Can you give me some insight?

D.L.
Memphis, TN

A I sat in the contact house with a grey-haired woman who wrote: "Your romantic relationship helped alleviate trust, but now you have blocked joy from coming into your life. To intellectualize your feelings is fine, but you should feel the range of emotions and then move on. That way, you can begin to reassess your past situations. You must learn to trust others; they don't have to prove themselves at all times. Your mother has been proving her love for many years. Maybe it is time to mother her a little. She will not allow it a lot as she is very locked into her way of life, but you can open yourself to love. Start with your mother, this will remove the blocks. As you start to let them down, you will be rewarded by friendship and kindness. Then you can move on to the male relationships you want. You must refrain from taking too much and not giving enough back." **—Adina Leigh**

As Adina finished, Abenda said she wanted to get two perspectives on love. She proceeded to call in two more guides who could give some information about past lives. The first one to appear was a distinguished-looking woman in her fifties who wanted to relate an important past life: "Adina is right. Deborah is suffering from being so loved in this life that she doesn't know when she needs to give back. She needs to realize that she can have anything she desires, but she needs to give some recognition to others. It's hard for her to do this because in her last life, she was the prime minister of Spain. She encouraged reform and tried to work in new laws and did very well. She got much help in that life and much respect, and even though she didn't give of herself emotionally, she gave politically in the service of others. She doesn't understand that she needs to let others love her without wanting to use this in a political, manipulating sort of way. She must trust that others like her for who she is and not for any other reason. If she works on it, this will come to pass very soon." **—Talynda Faulkner**

The second guide Abenda called was a tall, pretty woman clad in white robes who gave this past-life information: "Deborah had many incarnations as a serious student of art in Greece. She was very passionate and let her emotions come to the fore, but they were squelched by the karma she had with her husband and his ruthless family. They told her that she was a woman, and couldn't be an artist. They kept her from practicing her craft, so she became very discouraged. She should practice art in this life, for this is an area where she can again express her feelings." **—Bethany Agrippa**

Regrets and Dreams

Q Dear Tara: I am eighty-two years old, and it seems that the story of my life is that everything I do is wrong or turns out wrong. I am always getting ripped off. My whole life has been a big mess. I can't blame my mother for that. I wish I could tell her how sorry I am that I didn't treat her better when she was alive. I could have cared for her and treated her better; she had a hard life and did the best she knew how. The other thing I am truly sorry for is the way I treated my husband. He was a good man, but I was not a good wife. We were married only a short time. I wish I could tell him "I am sorry," but I don't believe he is still alive. My mother passed away in 1949, and I am all alone. I never remarried and I don't have any friends. I am partly disabled.

I need to move and there is a house up the street from me that I've always wanted to move into. It's just right for me but I don't have the money to buy it. I dream of living there but every time I think I've figured out a way to get the money, something goes wrong. Just recently, two young men robbed me. They took two steel security boxes that contained my life's savings and important legal documents. I am sorry to take up so much of your time with my sorrows, but I just had to talk to somebody.

M.C.
Bloomington, CA

 A very sweet, grey-haired woman greeted me. She said she was glad to be able to communicate with Mary and wrote: "Oh,

Mary, I have never gotten to say hello to you in this lifetime. You and I have been together many, many times and spent many years together. You are in a time of transition now. The boys who stole your belongings will suffer greatly for doing these things. I know it seems as though it is not a fair world, but all is a learning experience. I know it is very hard at your age, but you need to meet like-minded friends. You will meet a few younger friends who will be happy to assist you.

"As for saying you're sorry to your husband and your mother, all you need to do is say that you're sorry now and then forgive and like yourself. That is also the learning part of earth. You will now be able to release these tendencies and go on to a more positive outlook. I will be here for you, I am always your friend. Much love to you, dear." **—Matilda Lee**

> **Note from Abenda:** "Mary, you are on a good road and I see life fall into place for you. Remember to count your blessings and know that all is wondrous and beautiful. We all love you."

A Soap Opera Life

 Dear Tara: I feel as though I have run into a brick wall of chaos and frustration in every area of my life—personal, professional, emotional. My husband and I are stressed and arguing. He was seriously injured recently and required two operations and three hospitalizations. His injuries were the result of a violent crime committed against him. During all the stress about this, our young son has become very difficult and clingy. I am having problems at work with various co-workers and superiors. I am also having great difficulty operating any kind of machinery—car, washing machine, dryer—causing them to break and leading to disagreements with service people. My grandmother died recently, and I've gained weight and feel tired all the time.

Help! I'm living a soap-opera life! I want to know why I have to experience so many things all at one time. Before this time, my life had been full of love, joy, balance and energy. Now I feel like I have lost my center and nothing I do seems to help me regain it. Can you give me some insight as to what is going on?

D.M.
Stockton, CA

 A woman in flowing white robes held out her hand for the pen. She began to write immediately: "Dona must relax and not give in to the emotional imbalance of it all, knowing that if she can be positive, it will help to restore an energy balance. Life runs in cycles, but they pass and things change. If they will change for the better or worse is up to her, and how she reacts to her experiences. She needs to sleep, rest, eat, and be productive. It is also a trying time for the others in Dona's life as well. She can be a rock of Gibraltar to them and thus create much good karma. Believe me, life is much more miserable for many other people.

"She experienced similar circumstances in a lifetime in Rome. She had a nice life, full of love and caring, then her son was hurt and one disaster led to another. That life ended badly, which is why she's projecting chaos into this life, but it doesn't need to be. I want Dona to know that I will help bring her stability. If she will take from me the projection of stability, she can relax and have a good life." —**Petra Dama**

Abenda nodded at Petra's advice and added the following: "Breathe deeply and relax completely. You can do this anytime, anywhere. Imagine white light coming through your crown chakra and encompassing your body inside and out. Have the light then ground into the earth to steady yourself. This will help calm, ground and center you. Be strong. Things will get better if you let them"

She Sees Ghosts

Q Dear Tara: I have seen spirits ever since I was seven years old. I am now forty. I cannot explain the reason for being able to see them; perhaps it's because I have always been a very open-minded person. Every house that my family and I have ever lived in has always had different spirits that made their presence known to me. I see children, animal and adult spirits that often come up to my bedside at night. They don't appear every night, though. Sometimes I don't see them for a few weeks, and then they appear again. My children, Tara and Mandy, see them as well but not as often as I seem to.

I have never been able to communicate with them through automatic writing. Whenever I try, I never get a response. I have great patience and don't push for a response, but I would like to know if you could ask your guides if I have some kind of block or if there is something I could do to be able to communicate with these presences that live among us.

D.G.
Oakview, CA

A **Abenda wanted to write this before calling in Diane's guide:** "Diane, you and your children are of a very high attunement. Your auric hum is of a high vibration, which is why you can go through the dimension and see what you see. I will call in your guide later; I am sure it will be a light person. As for communicating with the ghosts that you see, you can see them but cannot contact them because they are a lower vibration. Instead, you should keep a journal of your sightings and their habits, etc. I know you aren't allowed to communicate—I'm sure communication is being blocked by your light beings—but you could always find someone else on the earth plane who has a lower vibration than yours who could translate and be aware enough to have full protection and help them to the light, for they are lost souls."

Abenda then called Diane's guide in to communicate and it was a light being who entered the room. I couldn't quite make out the name, but it sounded like Ergrazan. Here is the communication: "You are of our kind, sent back to help others. You have much to do still, as do your daughters. Your life is changing, but in very good directions. We are here to guide you. Do not be afraid, just know that we are here for you. You have many abilities you have not explored yet." **—The Light Being**

Friend Murdered

Q Dear Tara: I recently lost a good friend, as well as mentor, to what seems to be a senseless murder. I have been a police officer for eight years; my friend was a thirty-six-year veteran of the force. He was gunned down while assisting in the investigation of a homicide. Prosecution of the case is still pending, so I cannot reveal any details of the incident, however his transition to the other side has left an enormous void. As a crime scene expert, I was dispatched to the hospital to photograph and collect as much evidence as I could from his body. As I walked into the trauma room, the eyes of the medical staff were fixed on me. I looked at my friend's lifeless form on the table, and tears welled up and I began to shake. I blinked back the tears, donned a pair of surgical gloves, loaded my camera and began shooting pictures. As I was working, I could feel his presence in the room. For a brief moment, I felt happy for him, although I knew it was a terrible loss for the community as well as myself. Another crime scene expert arrived a short time later, and between the two of us, we were able to get the job done. The medical staff was wonderfully supportive and we drew strength from them.

As a police officer, I have witnessed man's inhumanity toward man in its worst form, yet somehow I have managed to maintain a healthy perspective. This incident, however, has brought out anger in me like I have never experienced before. As time has passed, this anger has turned into depression. My personal life has been marked by one tragedy after another, and now my professional life seems to be following the same tragic motif. My meditations, although relaxing, don't seem to answer my questions. I'm hoping you can utilize your skills and answer this question for me: Why do I create this reality for myself?

G.L.
Houston, TX

A **George's friend wrote this:** "Hi. I want to tell you that I'm well and doing fine here. It's okay that I am no longer there; sorry the dramatic departure depressed you—I was shocked at first too. I accomplished what I wanted with my life and I have plenty to do on this side. Use your psychic intuition more and don't be depressed. I need you to carry on and do good work for our people.

"We've had such a close bond because we've been together many times before. The last time we were soldiers in the trenches; you died first and left me holding the bag. I missed you then, too, but we will see each other again. I can see some things very clearly over here, though others are blurry. I can see this now: You will gain stature and prominence in the community. You must trust yourself—you have a good heart and avenues that you had thought closed will open wide. You will walk hand-in-hand with many brothers and help mankind. Your career will be going in positive directions; even my death will help you open psychic channels to be more and feel more. You are a great friend; I could ask for no better."

Abenda added this note: "You don't need to worry about your friend; he is doing extremely well. He has a very high vibrational tone and came right to the light. You are so much more empathic than you think you are. You must close yourself off occasionally, for you tend to be dragged down by negative energy. You can use your psychic abilities for your work. Experience only the knowledge, not the pain. You will go far in life."

What Lies Ahead?

 Dear Tara: My whole life has been a struggle: childhood poverty and hardships, illness throughout my life, seventeen hard years as a nun until I left in 1963, financial problems that were devastating at times. Life has been difficult, indeed, but I have also had a transformation in my life and have been raised to a higher level of consciousness since my health improved in 1983.

I moved two years ago to New Jersey to care for a dear friend I have known for the past fifteen years; he is one-hundred years old. Adolf has been very kind to me but I am so in need of some personal free time to pursue my goals and dreams. However, I feel indebted to Adolf, who has aided me financially and is providing for me after his transition. He is mentally and physically alert, and is capable of caring for himself, but he wants me to see him every day of the week and is upset if I ask for free time.

I wondered if you could contact a spirit guide to get some insight into my life and see what lies ahead for me. How grateful I would be for this information. Thank you so much for your kindness. I am gratefully yours,

V.T.V.
Hawthorne, NJ

 Abenda introduced me to a beautiful, silver-haired woman, who kissed me on the cheek. She said she was very happy to be able to communicate with Virginia and had this to say: "Dear Virginia, you are at the end of caring for your

friend. You will soon be set free to travel and experience some of the pleasures of life. You have always felt blocked from pleasure before. You were also a nun in a past life in Rome. Women are not treated as well as priests in that religion, for the hierarchy is for men only, so this made you unsatisfied with Catholicism. Now you find again that you have sought the solitude of being a nun in this life, being holy and seeking purity.

"You will consciously make further efforts to exert your outgoing ways so you can have what you feel fun should be, for fun and laughter is the purity of God. Crying and separateness is the shunning of God, so smell the flowers, laugh and open your heart to experience the goodness of others.

"You also had a life as a monk in Tibet; you loved that silent lifetime. Your family had been murdered and you staggered around until a monk found you and took you into the brotherhood. You were fearful of others after your family had been murdered and were grateful to enjoy the security of the monkhood. The incident left a residue of distrust of other's motives. You should trust your instincts. It is a blessing to be a good person, but now it is time for you to experience sunshine and laughter." **—Lucy Meinor**

> **Abenda added this note:** "You have set yourself apart from others with a barrier of solitude. It is time to visualize whole, happy, honest people coming into your life. Go forth among others and extend your hand in friendship and wisdom."

Needs Answers

Q Dear Tara: I need some help in determining what direction to go with my life. I also need help for my son, who can't seem to find his place in this world. He is very depressed and can't tolerate being bossed. He is loving but he rejects receiving love because he doesn't feel worthy. But I sit and cry because I don't have any answers to help him.

J.K.
Aurora, IL

A **Abenda called in Judy's guide, who wrote this:** "For your son not to be lost, you must direct him. Give him a set agenda and tell him to try and seek goodness in life. He is rejecting love now and wallowing in self-pity and negativity. Always hand him lists of alternatives. Something will spark his interest and he will find self-esteem. You suffer from lack of self-esteem too, and find solace and passion in food, which causes you to have burdens with your weight. Turn your passion outward, renew your zest for living and extend yourself to others. As you build your self-esteem by fulfilling your desires in life, look for ways to help your son attain his. First of all, what does he like to do for hobbies? Is it something you do together? Help him arrange to get more involved in it, but remember to be helpful, not to do it for him.

"You two have been together before. The last time was in South America, which was a very hard life. All you did was work to survive, so your son is confused as he has never accepted that life could be easier than the last time. Let me reassure you that you will soon find many expressions of joy." —**Barbara Wayside**

Note from Abenda: "Self-esteem can be a nuisance, can't it? It seems there is enough to worry about without having to lift yourself up by the collar and tell yourself to be good and kind to yourself. But you need to do it and you need to study and gain knowledge and grow. We need gentle reminders to have a happy life. Here is another gentle reminder for you: Live, learn and laugh."

A Bad Life?

Q Dear Tara: It seems I've have spent most of my life crying because I can't understand what I have done to have such a bad life, or why God let it happen to me. I was born sick and was sickly until 1986. I've had five major operations in my early thirties. I was abused emotionally, physically and sexually as a child. My mother died when I was two, and my sister and I were separated. She lived not far away from me, but whenever she saw me, she would beat me up. I made my first suicide attempt at the age of six—I drank a whole bottle of iodine because I saw the skull and crossbones on it, and thought it would kill me. All that happened was that I threw up a lot of blood for a couple of days. No one noticed, which was usual, and I was afraid to tell anyone so I wouldn't get beaten. There are many more things I could tell you. I could go on for pages. I want to know, what did I do to cause such a life, and how can I improve it? It has started to improve somewhat since I began studying metaphysics in 1986, but there are so many things I don't understand.

L.W.
Chicago, IL

A tall, slender woman reached for the pen to reassure Liana: "Liana, honey, it is okay to feel like life dealt you a bad hand. But life is looking up for you now. You have love and peace. Now you will gain understanding.

"You chose this lifetime because you were a German Jew in Auschwitz in your last life. You reincarnated too quickly after that lifetime, which is why you were born so sickly and suffered so much until 1986. The physical effects carried over from the concentration camp into this lifetime, but your spirit has healed now. Because you were persecuted in that incarnation, you chose to be born black in this lifetime—another persecuted race of people—but you chose to be born in America, the land of freedom and opportunity.

"I was your African mother in a life in the 1500's; we had a happy life then and I love you still. Because I was your mother then, and since you lost your mother early in this life, I will love you and guide you as a mother.

"You must start working on your self-esteem. Start by knowing that you are the best and smartest and prettiest and most perfect human being! You can give up false assumptions generated by simple minds and know that you deserve all of life's pleasures.

"Karma is karma; you have overcome all that pain and sadness. You have come forward bravely through difficulties, and you will continue in a positive direction, filled with life and love." —**Jennifer Bambinaso**

Abenda wrote this: "The rest of your life will be good. Don't be afraid; know that love and peace conquer all injustice and fear."

Wants To Commit Suicide

 Dear Tara: I will have hope for the first time in my life if you can answer my question about suicide. I feel if it's our time to go on and there's no other way, then suicide is the answer.

When I was twenty-seven, I had the following experience: I was at the dentist's office. When they put me out, I floated up to the ceiling. I was looking down at my husband and three kids. I wanted to go on up, but someone was there with me, stopping me. They told me I had babies to take care of and would come later.

That was twenty-two years ago. Every day since, I ask God if now is the day I can go. I long for the day I will be brave enough to end it all. Because my financial obligations are so great, my insurance will not pay them all, so now I have to wait two more years before I can commit suicide. That's if I can do it. I'm so sad; I feel like I missed my date with God to go on to better things. Can you please tell me that it's okay to kill myself?

                                                        A.C.
                                            Grand Rapids, MI

Abenda said she would answer for the guide as well as herself: "You do **not** want to commit suicide. Everyone on the earth plane must realize that you become very confused and lower your vibrational pattern when you give up your gift of life.

"If someone is dying of cancer and has only three weeks to live, quickening the death process is not so bad; you lower your vibration very little. But if you just feel like doing yourself in, well, that isn't a good enough cause to give up the body. These are tests you must face. Even positive karma victims fear life; karmic tests can be very, very hard.

"If you so truly desire to die, you are not doing enough in life that brings your self-esteem to a worthwhile level. If you want to see pain, start volunteering at some cancer clinics, AIDS hotlines, downtown homeless programs—there are many organizations and you may find a job that will give you some purpose in life.

"If your perspective is that life can be hard, I want to tell you that death can be just as harsh and hard, especially at the lower vibrations. Don't fool yourself—the higher you can raise your vibration, the more you fulfill your soul's purpose, which is to return to the Godhead. Suicide only prolongs the process. You committed suicide in your last life, and some of its lower vibration still clings to you in this life. You must rise above it and face life."

Out of Work

 Dear Tara: I have been out of work for over a year. I have been doing a lot of meditation to direct my energies toward working with horses. I love horses very much and want them to be part of my life once more. I have sent resumes all over California, but because I don't have any current experience, I'm not getting any responses to them. I'm willing to start out working in the stable. My current background is in property management, and I have owned my own mechanical construction business. I am willing to incorporate my management skills, and have stated this in the cover letter I send with my resumes.

I haven't given up my faith, but I am getting weary. My home is in foreclosure and I don't know which way to turn.

D.W.
Long Beach, CA

 Abenda introduced me to a man who called himself "Donna's guiding angel." He said he was happy to share this guidance with Donna: "In your last incarnation, you chose a very stable life, but you craved adventure, travel and excitement. In this life, you are a woman again, but this time you have to work hard for stability. And now you are assuring yourself of adventures. Try not be stressed. Enjoy your options. Opportunities will open to you and you will enjoy your life as soon as it settles down. That's when you will find a new job. It will be helping others, and you will feel of service and be fulfilled. Good luck on all this; I am with you on all these adventures of life."

—Fred Barnes, your guiding angel

Abenda added this note: "You can program your life the way you want it to be. Exercise your talents and do not wait for an occupation to come to you. You are the one who creates your own reality. Do it."

Chapter Six

Death, Dying and Communication

We all fear death—fear moving on into the unknown because it is unknown. We seem to have purposely blocked all knowledge of our natural home on the other side of the veil.

My automatic writing experiences lead me to believe that the spirit world is a definite place, every bit as real as the earth plane, maybe more so. My altered-state experiences on the other side confirm those written about by other authors, researchers, and seekers. I retain my full range of physical senses "over there." The light, so often talked about, is white, not sunshine yellow. The entities I see are translucent from the knees up, yet I can touch them and they feel solid. Language is never a problem in the nonphysical realms. Although I can only speak English and Spanish in my current body, it appears that all languages are universal—words project essence, which is easily perceived. I do, however, ask that my automatic writing come through in English.

Abenda has said many times, "Dying doesn't make you smarter." Awareness and vibrational advancement is the result of growth achieved while on the earth plane— "spiritual brownie points," I sometimes say. The more we are able to rise above our fear-based emotions and unconditionally love humankind, the more brownie points we receive. Abenda screens the discarnate entities desiring to communicate with the living. When a confused or unaware entity is allowed to "write," it is only to relate personal experiences from their perspective. I also like to point out that no discarnate with a vibrational rate lower than your own can influence you in any way unless you invite them in. Abenda and Rod will explain.

I've found great comfort in knowing my friends on the other side, and in being allowed to glimpse what "life" will be like after death. My spiritual guides have explained it is my dharma to light a path of awareness for others—to help people understand the reasons for their experiences and to rise above their fear of death. It isn't something I set out to do. It's still difficult for me to accept that I am doing it, and at the same time, nothing I've ever done has felt as natural or brought me such peace.

From Rod Invergordon: "There are many who never hear or feel their guides until they cross over. And there are others who, even though guide contact is very privileged, have to close down their channels of communication because they cannot handle two realities at once. And many others get scattered with the dual energy when they do not ground themselves with earth reality.

"The lower astral plane is a slow vibrational rate. Entities of a lower frequency get trapped by the vibrational pull. This is the phenomenon you see in haunted houses; these are entities that are so low that they remain earthbound and can't complete their transition. They have no power over the living unless you allow them to lower your own vibration through negative thoughts and actions. This is also why it is important to let go of any guilt and not to succumb to alcohol or drug addiction. If you dwell on your miseries, you pull in those entities who sympathize with your miseries. This comforts them and only makes you feel even more miserable. Be careful, protect yourself with cheerfulness, happiness, prayers, mantras or white light."

From Abenda: "Death is still very much a live state to those of us who are dead. We just communicate in a different way. Tara has means to communicate with those of us on this side of the veil. I am happy that I can communicate so easily with Tara, but this is what we planned at her inter-council meeting.

"As for your guides and how you set up your life, you know that if you work at knowing your guides, you can. It is easier for some to contact their guides; others find it very hard to communicate and trust they are reaching their guide. You know if it is a bad connection when you are told to act, think or behave negatively. Guides want only the best for the person they watch over. How evolved the guide is depends on their evolution while on the earth, but as a guide, they are always set in a positive alignment to assist those on the earth. When you experience a good conscience, it is your guide leading you away from a situation that would bring stress or pain.

"Guides also meet the souls of those they guide at the time of death, although you may not recognize them for a while. It depends on how you are feeling and the circumstances regarding the death sequence. You should prepare for your death in ways that will make it as painless as possible. The best advice I can give you is not to worry excessively about death. When it happens, the process is very quick, and you make the choice to leave the body and go to the light. Actually, death is a very euphoric state for a while, although there are some people who miss the body and the feelings and begin to panic. That is why the guides are there, to help you through the transition stage. There is nothing you can do anyway but go on, experience your life with insight, and start to move further into the light.

"As far as entity attachment is concerned, they cannot attach themselves unless you allow them too. This can happen only if you have holes in your aura and allow it. Depression, anger, drugs, and alcohol can bring this about. You need to center yourself and put a lot of white light around your body and mind."

World War I Pilot

Q Dear Tara: I began having a very strange psychic experience in 1986 that involved a World War I pilot. I saw his photograph at a restaurant and felt an immediate, overwhelming sense of recognition and love. I became obsessed with learning everything I could about him and even bought the photo from the restaurant. After months of research, I learned his identity. I also discovered several startling facts. We share the same backgrounds, career interests and even hobbies. Many important dates in his life correlate with important dates in mine. The most intriguing thing I discovered was that he died twelve hours before I was born. I have undergone hypnosis, visited psychics and even wrote a fictional account of the experience. I felt very close to this man. Years have passed, but I still wonder what the purpose of the experience was.

J.H.
Los Angeles, CA

A **A young man balanced the notepad on his knee and wrote the following:** "Yes, you are the reincarnation of your pilot. I knew you well in that lifetime. You felt most free when you were flying, but in this lifetime you have gone on, no longer worrying about the freedom and calling of the guard.

" You must continue to try to sell your book; people will like the theme. You no longer hold onto the war memory; you have this life to fulfill. You can let go of your earlier life now. There will be a few more instances in your life that will bring you tremendous recognition and you won't have to experience pain first-hand. You no longer hold onto any depression or longing, so your life this time is good. You will thrive in the light." — **Mark Ingram**

Friend's Suicide

Q Dear Tara: Heather and I met in high school in the '60s and became instant friends. We shared a special bond—an attraction to the "Camelot" era in the Middle Ages. We were so close and did so many things together that we could read each other's minds. Later we moved away from each other, but we always kept in touch and retained that special connection.

After not seeing Heather for fifteen years, we met again in 1986 and spent the entire night talking. It seemed that we talked about everything, but in retrospect we didn't, because two weeks later I received the devastating news that she had committed suicide. Her mother, husband and children were shocked; nobody had known there were any problems, so none had seen it coming.

Though it was several years ago, her suicide still haunts me. How could we have talked all night without my realizing that she was in trouble? Why couldn't she tell me when we had always been so close? We were like soulmates, and I feel a void and a deep need to know why she killed herself. The headstone on her grave says, "Starting Over." I could accept her new start a little easier if only I knew why.

**R.J.
Norwood, CO**

I observed Heather as she walked through the garden toward us. She wore a black hat and navy style peacoat, and her hair was disheveled. This is what she wrote: "Rhonda, I'm very sorry that I upset you so. I hadn't meant to do that to anyone. I did mean to kill myself, but since I am no longer there to watch my children grow and see what my life could have been, I'm sad for that. Depression seemed to tug at me, I really felt like my life was hanging by threads, and I was filled with doubts and worries. I wanted out of all my responsibilities and the pain that comes with them. You are to live more bravely than I did. Please don't doubt yourself."

Abenda suggested bringing in one of Heather's guides. When the woman appeared, Heather called her "Mother." I questioned this and Heather explained that the woman had been her mother in another life. Mother was a very austere woman in her forties. This is what Mother wrote: "Yes, well, the girl I've come to fetch was indeed hasty, and she had an even rangier lifetime in the hills of Tennessee with me and many siblings. We were dirt poor and her pa died early on. But we kept surviving and she went and ran off with this shoe-shine boy, and he gave her lots of babies without marrying her. He finally left her with those children and they were hard put for all their life. She must have panicked in her very last life, because I thought she had it pretty good."

Since Heather has been wandering the swampland of her own creation for years, Abenda and I talked to Heather's mother about taking her to the

light. Mother told Heather, "You want to walk in marshes, do it on a higher level, where you can relax and visit some folks that can help you."

Abenda added this note: "Heather's Tennessee incarnation was overburdened with responsibility and she was miserable; things in that life never improved for her. In this life, she subconsciously feared her responsibilities would bring the same result. She couldn't cope with the idea of no light at the end of the tunnel. The fear wasn't valid in her current life, but she didn't recognize that so the fear was undiminished. Situations like this demonstrate how wrong it is to judge others for what they do. Rhonda, your inquiry may have helped Heather find peace. She would have eventually accepted help on her own, but maybe we accelerated the process."

Can't Contact Sister

Q Dear Tara: My question is about my sister, who killed herself when I was twenty-one. Our mother died of cancer when we were young and we both felt the loss very deeply. I was able to contact my mother on the other side, who reassured me she is well and happy now that she is free of the cancer. She said she was sorry to miss this lifetime but she is with me always and we are one. I have repeatedly tried to contact my sister on the other side, but I get nothing. I feel that we're still connected and she's okay, but I get no response from her. Can you help me?

S.L.
Pensacola, FL

Abenda sat on the couch next to a young woman who wrote: "It is hard for me to write, I can't really write yet. Please help me. I feel as though I made circumstances worse for myself by dying. And I didn't even have a bad life; I was just very confused and felt no one cared. My mother died and left me emotionally distraught. I still feel that way even though she calls me every day to please come see her. But I must swim through murky turbulence, and again I am a coward, so I cannot see her, and she will not come down to the depths of my existence to see me. I hope to get over my depression soon. If not, I do not know what to do. I am so barren of joy." **—Your Loving Sister**

A woman came in and hugged the girl, then wrote the following: "She was shocked to see me. She finds it hard to believe I am really here. I have come to try and take her above. She has come this far, I must take her with me. Do not weep, my baby, for I am here to comfort and guide you. I will look after you and help you feel better about yourself. I want to say that I thank Stacy for her assistance in bringing her sister to me. She feels helpless and alone.

"My daughter and I shared a life in Mexico during the 1800s. She was my sister, and we laughed and shared hopes and dreams. One day she caught a fever and died a few days later. I died a few years later, and then we were together again on the other side. We planned to be mother and daughter in this lifetime, and she knew I would die when she was very young. But when I did die, she couldn't handle it. I was happy to leave, but I didn't mean for my dear children to suffer so. I am so glad to

have this opportunity to talk to you, Stacy, and I want to thank you again for reuniting the three of us in this way. I will try and care for your sister. Do have joy in life."
—**Mom**

As the mother and daughter sat with their arms around each other, talking, Abenda took the pen and added this note: "Predestined circumstances can heal or make life and death painful. You need to balance all the good and bad in life. Appreciate the good and hold onto it.

"Stacy, know that your love and concern have brought your sister the first strands of light through the dark veil. Suicide can be a predestined possibility also, but suicide confuses the person who takes that way out, and their soul remains depressed for a while. Those who commit suicide need extra prayers so they will hear the positive callings to the light. They can't seem to lift themselves out of the depths of their own darkness and fear."

Inherited Business

Q Dear Tara: My father died a year and a half ago. Sometimes I feel like I understand and then I'm angry because I don't know what to do about the family business he left. No one wants to listen to me. I'm thirty-two years old but everyone thinks I'm too young to handle things. I also have to help my alcoholic brother. I'm so confused about my father's death. I'm sick all the time with stomach and gallbladder problems. Can you please help me?

C.M.
Fargo, SD

The room was empty at first, then Abenda entered, followed by two young men. The first one wrote this: "Cheri, you are learning the hard way, but it is a good road you are traveling in this life. Your dad did not mean for his company to be a burden; he is glad you are able to handle this responsibility, and he is very proud. He wishes he could hug you and tell you how proud he is. His message to you is to accept help from others but maintain control. Ask for truthful opinions but don't go by everyone's word. Ask others in the same business for pointers and take workshops that will help you learn to handle procedures. You mustn't pity yourself; you will learn to work it all out. You have a very big gift in this situation, maybe even an overwhelming gift, but in the long run you will be thankful." —**Larry Leede**

The second young man said he was there to tell you about past lives. He wrote: "During one lifetime, in France, you owned a boutique and a beauty parlor. You had two sons who ran these stores for income after you died. One son had a very hard time but the other son managed well. He took over the other brother's store and brought both businesses to a high standing. The son who managed well was your father in this life; the son who failed became your brother in this life. Your brother needs to learn to help himself, but he also needs help so that he can function as a whole person. He has been emotionally crippled for too many lifetimes. You have a wonderful opportunity to run this business, so you must do what you must for yourself. You are strong; you can run it." —**Harrison**

Abenda added this note: "Cheri, you need to view this situation as a learning experience. You will attain far more with emotional maturity in the long run. Trust yourself and always be fair and honest. Take this opportunity to learn and grow."

Brother Has AIDS

Q Dear Tara: Three months ago, my twenty-nine-year-old brother, who is also my best friend, discovered that he has AIDS. It has progressed rapidly and he is in the final stages of the disease at this point. He is not gay, has never been an IV drug user nor had a transfusion. I am having a lot of trouble accepting the fact that he has this horrible disease and that he will die of it. I pray for the wisdom and strength to carry on once he has passed. I'm hoping that I will see him again, that our paths will cross on a different plane. Is there anything you can suggest to help my anxiety and sense of loss? I respect your insights. Thank you.

E.W.
San Francisco, CA

A **Abenda wrote the following:** "It is so very hard to let go of a loved one when they cross over to the other world. You are not alone among all who mourn love lost. But it is never lost, only added to the records of future love. Your brother himself chose to have this disease, as have many souls on the earth plane. He is releasing many future lifetimes of hardship by accepting this hardship in this life. Others around him have been affected by his sacrifice, and in his way, he has helped many.

"Beloved is beloved. You will mourn for him, but you can be comforted he will be as whole as you are in another dimension of time and space. You are not to worry, as the love you share will find you once again together. Store the gifts he has given you in your heart. I will call in someone who can tell you more about the past lives concerned."

As Abenda finished writing, a young woman entered the room and identified herself as your brother's guide. She wanted to tell you this: "Your brother is fine now. You must know that he loves you very much and is very sorry to put his family through such pain and sadness.

"His karma is his own; in some ways, it had nothing to do with you and in other ways, it would stir up your compassion to give of yourself to others. He was a soldier in his last life, and even though he was not gung ho at hurting others, he felt very guilty for following orders. His karma will strengthen him for more ideal lives in the future." **—Nancy**

Sister Is Dying

Q Dear Tara: I have a sister who is severely diabetic. Her kidneys failed and she is on dialysis. Recently she developed pneumonia, and I'm afraid she is slipping away and will die soon. Because she is on SSI, the doctors are very uncooperative and treat her very callously. I love her dearly and suffer her pain and frustration with her. I don't want to lose her. I have been praying unrelentingly for a healing. Together, we have investigated every possible avenue for her healing, including hypnosis, mega-nutrients, crystals, positive thinking, faith healing, etc. She's been to doctors from Boston to Houston, but we've had no luck, and now this. Can your guides offer any help?

T.P.
Houston, TX

A **Abenda brought two women who were willing to address this painful subject for Tisa. One named Rosa decided to write first:** "Your sister is in horrible pain. She needs to come back to this side to rejuvenate her spirit as her physical body has tortured her. She set this up for herself, of course, but so much has happened already that on a superconscious level, she has no real will to live. It is not surprising that this is so. You need to tell her how much you love and cherish her, but that you will understand if she leaves you behind. You are terribly afraid to be left alone, and she wants so much to stay and finish this life with you.

"You must remember that she will always live on. You have lived many lifetimes together and you will live many lives together in the future. Gain peace and understanding. As unfair as life may seem, remember that you have had a beloved sister who loved you dearly. There are many who do not have this unconditional love and acceptance." **—Rosa Maine**

The other woman wrote this: "You have had many incarnations together. In one, you were Roman centurions together, the best of friends. You went into battle with him, were badly wounded and died in his arms. He was grateful that he could be there for you so you could die in the arms of someone who loved you so much.

"In an American Indian lifetime, the two of you were drinking at a stream when a bear came after you. You sacrificed yourself so he could get away. He felt very guilty about this, and was deeply anguished over your absence.

"In this life, your sister is leaving first so she doesn't have to confront the pain of losing you again. You have sacrificed for her in many lifetimes; in this life, she must die first while she is young so as not to outlive you. This is not necessarily rational, but sometimes this is what we do with our karma when we are deciding our lives. She is compounding all the old debts so that in the future, she can live wonderful long and healthy lifetimes. Whether this happens depends on how brave she is. Be there for her, tell her you love her." **—Frances Meyer**

Was Father Murdered?

 Dear Tara: I hope you can help me with this problem. My father died in 1966, and the state ruled that he committed suicide. This has been very traumatic for my whole family, especially two of my sisters. They both suffer grave emotional and mental disorders. Many years later, I checked again with the coroner, off the record, and he told me he had always felt it was a homicide. Can you ask your guides to tell me what the truth is about this? Maybe I can help my sisters with this knowledge in some way.

G.H.
Honolulu, HI

 A woman shook my hand and said she would be glad to help straighten this out. She sat on the couch and proceeded to write the following: "Your father had been arguing with someone about something work-related. Your father was working late one night and this man came to his office. He came to confront your father about something your father knew. Your father would never have harmed this man with his knowledge of his wrong-doing, but the man didn't realize this. He lost his temper when your father wouldn't agree to something and killed him. It was entirely a spur-of-the-moment crime, not intentional, so the man was able to cover it up. The family had met the killer, but only a few times. He was a thin man with medium brown hair, and stood about six feet tall.

"In one life they shared, they were Indians in a very cold country hunting for food. One day, a bear was attracted by a moose they had killed. The other man decided to try to kill the bear, but your father wanted to give up the kill and refused to help the other man. The other man died and your father was able to get away. He was sorry, but felt that to give up the kill was the best thing to do.

"In another shared lifetime, in mid-nineteenth century Texas, the other man was a lawman. Your father was a supplier who cheated people in subtle ways. When the lawman confronted your father with his cheating, your father hit him on the head with a rock, and the man died. Your father dragged the lawman out of town and let his horse go. The townspeople thought the lawman had fallen off the horse and died, so they did not investigate.

"It seems that your father and this man share accidental-type karma, coming together to do each other in. Basically, they don't hate each other, they just act out the karma. They need to forgive each other and learn from their pain; it's time for a rest.

"You will be with your father again. He loved you and is sad he had to leave you. He is fine now. You and your sisters must carry on. You must continue to love and hope, and know that death is only a transition."
—Betty Kay Lewis

> **Note from Abenda:** "We're all here to experience pain and joy—that is what the earth plane has to offer. The circumstances of your karma either makes you into a better, more positive person, or it breaks you down into a more negative, fearful person. Only you can choose and decide how this will work for you."

Am I Her Mother?

 Dear Tara: I held my mother in my arms as she died last year. After urging her to follow the light and telling her goodbye, I found myself stroking her head and thinking, "I brought her into this world, and now I have seen her out of it." I felt very ancient and peaceful. Then I wondered, is this why I had such a burning desire to be with her when she crossed over?

After years of exploring past lives, I'm sure I was my mother's mother. My grandmother was in her early twenties when she died in 1918 during the Asian flu epidemic. She died holding her one-year old daughter. I was born thirty years later.

My grandfather died three days after my grandmother, leaving three orphaned children. Throughout her long life, my mother looked forward to meeting her parents "in heaven." And here I am, still on earth and wondering, am I her mother? If so, how does she feel about me not being there in heaven to greet her?

In meditation, I've tried to communicate with her, but I only sense her loving attempts to comfort me and her exuberance over her present state. Can you clarify this?

K.C.
Woodland Hills, CA

 Your mother said she had much to share with you. This is what I received from her: "It is very good to have made a connection with you so that Katherine and I can communicate. I want to tell her how wonderful it was to ease out of that world and into this one as she held me in her arms. I didn't realize that she was my very own mother until attaining the knowledge over here. I know now that she didn't mean to leave me as my mother. It was a situation we both had to experience. When she was reborn as my daughter she always tried to make up for it. She helped me overcome the feeling of being abandoned and not being loved. I will be more than happy to love her for the rest of eternity.

"Although I was prepared to go, it was so hard to leave my family. Katherine is still fighting herself on that. She has guilt over wanting a life away from her parents.

"The reason my mother died when I was so young, is that in her former life all her children died in a horrible famine. She was so fearful of experiencing that pain of loss again, she checked out early. This time Katherine feels enormous pain over my death, and I comfort her, but I know she doesn't hear me. I don't want my family to be afraid of death. It is just a transition, not a true going away. I did look forward to meeting my mother over here, but I have learned what I had was far greater.

I want my family to know I loved them for all their support and love, especially in those last hard years. My memories of their smiles and laughter will always ring in my heart." —**Mother**

In my temple room, Katherine's mother gave me a hug.

Abenda added, "You know Katherine is kind and loving to all on the earth. She has been very disappointed by her fellow man and the why's of hurt and disease on the earth plane. In time, she will go into some form of human services to help nurture others through their pain."

Son Killed In Accident

Q Dear Tara: On May 19, 1988, my beloved son James was working temporarily in Marietta, Georgia. That night, he walked across the street to phone his wife Karen in Chicago. They argued and she hung up on him. He started back across the street and was struck by a car and killed.

I have been deeply and permanently saddened to have lost him so young and so tragically. I can't bear it when his little son looks at me with huge sad eyes, so much like his father's and asks, "Grandma, why did Daddy have to die?" Was it karma? Just a tragic accident? His destiny?

His wife Karen can't get on with her life. She feels so much guilt for hanging up on him that night. Our entire family is devastated. I've had music-related dreams about him (he was an aspiring musician), and he just looks at me and smiles a sweet, sad smile. In my dreams he looks so thin and sad. Can you get some answers for us? We would be eternally grateful.

C.A.H.
Toledo, OH

 James sat in the contact house, happy to make contact with his mother again. This is what he had to say: "I wasn't looking where I was going. What can I say? I'm sorry I hurt everybody. But I've just been hanging out, and I have this really bad leg that got mangled in the accident. I will try and change that. I like to hang out in Southern towns. Checking them out. I try not to get wrapped up in the family thing too much. I'm sorry my wife and I had a fight, but her hanging up on me had nothing to do with the accident. I didn't feel anything when I was hit, but it was an ugly sight from where I watched above. I didn't want to deal with all that, so I took the escape route.

"I miss my family and some friends, but I'm okay here. I don't have any past lives that I want to relate to as why it had to happen. Not that the lifetimes don't exist, I'm just not interested. I don't care about those things. Tell my mom, 'Hi,' and although the rest aren't much into this, love to them too."

> **Abenda then wrote:** "James is earthbound. Have his mother send him white light and love, and direct him to follow the lighted path. His guide will help him to find peace and direct him on that side. He is quite content to just 'hang around' but it doesn't serve him. He's not interested in talking with me so maybe his mother can help to show him the way."

I told Abenda that I wasn't satisfied with this information because I hadn't learned "why." I asked Abenda to bring James' spirit guide. A few moments later, a woman with shoulder-length reddish hair named Ranusa entered the room. This is what Ranusa wrote through my hand: "James' early death relates to his karma from several incarnations. In a Roman lifetime, he left his children then came back to them late in life expecting their help. In a Polish incarnation, he had an affair with an officer's wife and the officer had him slain. As a policeman in 1920s London, he worked among the clubs and longed to be able to entertain others. The wife of the Polish officer was his wife in the current life. His mother loves him and they are very much a part of each other's reincarnational lineage.

"It is proving difficult to get Jim off the earth plane, because he wants to remember the music and songs.

"It is difficult for me to relate to you how this all interrelates. I have a band set up over here to help him make another higher connecton. Jim is yelling at me now to go away. Soon, I will have to send another guide to coax him. Be of good mind and happy spirit." **—Ranusa**

Seven People Die

Q Dear Tara: Never in my life had I experienced the death of someone close to me, but from August of 1990 to September of 1991, I mourned the deaths of seven people, all either members of my family or close friends. At that time, I was pregnant with my second child.

The most difficult one for me was the death of my beautiful mother in March of 1991. Her absence has created an enormous void in my life. All I've ever wanted to do was to give her the happiness that she so much deserved. She'd had a very hard life—she was a survivor of World War II, physical abuse, abandonment, an alcoholic husband, life in a foreign country and much sacrifice for her children.

Every day, I feel the overwhelming need to hold her,

take care of her and make her happy. It haunts me terribly. I need guidance in understanding why I have this aching need that can't possibly be fulfilled. I miss her so terribly much. I wonder if she is happy. Does she know how much I appreciated her and how deep my love for her is?

Thank you so much for your time and guidance.

A.W.
Little Rock, AR

A **tall, dark-haired man moved forward to answer Anna's question:** "You are blessed, Anna. Know that your mother is happy and loves you very much. She didn't want to add to anyone's grief, but it was her time to leave. She had experienced all that she needed to experience on the earth plane, and she had chosen to leave before she could become a burden. She is in a very happy way here.

"You are on a journey, you know, and you have much to tell others. You have been blessed by knowing that your loved ones don't really die, they merely transform their energy and continue to live on another plane. You will soon have to talk to groups on the subject of grief. When you love someone as much as you loved your mother, it is painful to lose the physical touch and loving ways of that person. But you can use your own experience to counsel others who have suffered similar losses, who are grieving for others, and thus you can alleviate your own grief. You are not alone." **—Max Brikan**

Abenda had this to say: "To grieve is to release the sorrow of the soul. There is a turning point in grieving where you begin to keep that person alive in your heart. This is very healing, for to love and be loved is a true gift. On the material plane, your karma may not allow you to keep the love in a physical sense, but in most ways you can store it within yourself and be nurtured by it."

A girl took the pen from Abenda to add this note: "Your vibration is very close in tone to your mother's, and you have both chosen to share many loving lives with each other. You have been siblings in some lives and parents to each other in other lives. You will love each other always, for your karma together is positive. All relationships have high and low points, but this relationship has always been on an even roll." **—Afila**

Why Did My Father Hate Me?

 Dear Tara: As I was coming out of a meditation session, I was directed to ask you about my father. We never had a very good relationship. He had even a worse relationship with his father—by the time he was six years old, he'd had almost every bone in his body broken. When he was seventeen, he was in World War II. Though he and my mother seemed happy for many years, he died an alcoholic at fifty-five.

I need to understand why he hated me. Although he passed away six years ago, I've had a feeling lately that he hasn't gone to the light but is in limbo somewhere. He died so full of anger and hatred that I fear for him.

My father's name was Arlen.

B.G.

Arlen seemed very agitated and grabbed the notepad to jot this down: "What do you mean by disturbing me? I'm a very busy man. I don't want to face this."

Abenda explained that he should release the past. His response was: "Why??? It is too painful for me to even begin to think of it over here. I know I'm dead, but I don't care. I don't want to be disturbed about such things. Really, my way of dealing with this is to let it pass through my mind and never again have the thought."

Abenda asked him to remain and listen to what a guide had to say to him. He agreed, and a woman in her forties appeared. She wrote this: "His father was mad at the world. He had suffered many lifetimes by the hand of a desert tribe in the mountains in Olam. I know that his father too was very angry when united to the earth. Maybe he too can release some of this anger. You can ask him."

Abenda then called in Arlen's father and the two men stood scowling at each other. The grandfather wrote: "Babuhls was a good warrior, but he became sad for others and let our prisoners go. For this, he was sentenced to death, and the men all tortured him. Last time, on earth, he was born to me as we have shared many incarnations, but he refused to listen to my guidance. So it angered me and I chose to make sure he listened to me in the future.

"I love and hate this warrior, as he has been my close comrade and now he is an enemy. I couldn't let him destroy the plans and release prisoners. Besides, I am not sorry, but yet I am, because he came into the earth as my flesh and blood. But I couldn't help myself. He will not see me now. And we cannot work it out. And I fear I am not ready to take the steps again in an earth time. We cannot even get along here where we know and feel more."

At this point, Arlen wanted to write again: "He is right. It makes me sad to see him. I cannot even begin to let this go. He wants us to be friends again, but he must always have the last word, and I fear all that earthly pain and humiliation again. I do not believe in hurting flesh. I want all to get along, even if you have to repress those feelings. That's what I wanted for my family–peace at all costs. I didn't want to start any chain of events.

"My guilt from all my military incarnations has left me tired and wanting to experience life in a different way. That's if I ever go back to the earth. I fear hurting anyone else. Maybe I am miserable for it. I can't go on yet. I know there are higher levels and there are nice things where I am, but I don't deserve those yet. If I know Banklor will be far away, maybe I can go with this woman. But at this time even he doesn't follow me where I go."

When we were alone, Abenda wrote: "I find it very sad that two entities who find their way to each other express such resistance. Obviously, it was a painful life for Chris' father on many levels–deep levels of subconscious guilt and tragedy. We must work for the best even when we have been wronged or our karma is not easy. If you work on bettering your karma, it will improve. Send your father light and love, and work at forgiving him. Rather than hating you, your father was so fearful that fear was all he could express in life. You need to remember that your karma with him was the result of your own karmic configuration requiring this kind of challenge. Until you can forgive, you won't have fulfilled a major karmic opportunity."

Is My Guide My Mother?

Q Dear Tara: Recently, I made contact with my guides, which was very exciting, but I was told something that did not make me happy. The guide told me her name is Anna, and she is my "natural" mother.

I was adopted at an early age, and I have always hoped to meet my real mother some day. I did not expect to meet her as a guide. I have no way to verify my experience. It was very real, but I haven't been able to make contact again. Would you ask Abenda to verify my experience?

M.H.
Bermuda Dunes, CA

A **Abenda and two other women were on the couch when I entered the room. One of the women was Anna. She seemed like a person you could easily approach and talk to. She wrote:** "It is hard for me to even speak to you. I know that I failed you, and I failed myself in that way. I always wondered about you, but knew I had done the right thing. Especially considering I just didn't ever manage to get my life together. After giving you up, I had self-confidence problems and doubted my ability to do anything right."

Abenda wrote: "Anna is indeed your mother. She really loved you, but it was not accepted by society to have a child out of wedlock. It broke her heart when she turned you over to the nurse. She wanted to be your guide so she could help you as she could not in life."

A woman named Masica came in to write to you: "You knew her in a French lifetime. You wanted her to go with you, but we forbade it. So you left. She felt sad and lonely always, for you also. You must meet again and refuse to leave each other if you hope to work this out. Just continue to send love and she will too, so that someday you can be together."

Is The Time of Death Predetermined?

Q Dear Tara: Seven months ago, my beautiful twenty-four-year-old daughter died suddenly. She had a cardiac arrest and was gone. The autopsy showed no reason for her death. She was a happy, energetic young woman. She didn't do drugs and was very aware, taking care to eat properly.

I need to know if you believe the time and the way to die is determined in the plan or if our free will determines this after we are here? Edgar Cayce believed it is all determined before birth.

T.R.
Medford, OR

 A Abenda told me that your daughter was still earthbound and we drew her to us. She was still quite upset, but an older, white-haired

woman named Pepita soothed her. When she felt calmer, this is what your daughter wrote: "I didn't want to leave any of my family. I see you and know you miss me and I miss you so much. I am with you, but you don't see or hear me, and I've been very angry and hurt about it. I didn't mean to leave so quickly. I felt compelled to go with my experiences. It was like a dream, and then I couldn't come back into my body. I know everything is really okay. I also know that I am dead. I wish I could have said good-bye before I left. I want to hug you and tell you that you were the greatest. I love you. I'm near you." **—Patricia**

> **Abenda added this**: "Yes, we choose our own time to go. She knows she planned it, but is so attached to her grief that she has to be counseled by those chosen to help her, those she has a connection with. As for when and how you die, everyone on the earth plane has put in their order. How they handle the outcome is not known until after the fact."

Before they said good-bye, Pepita said she had something she wanted to tell Terri: "You and your daughter had a life together in Egypt as husband and wife. You were very close, but you got pneumonia and died. Patricia was the wife, and she longed for her husband all the rest of her life.

"In another lifetime, they were on the Mongolian front line as a small band of warriors. Again, Terri died first and Patricia mourned for a very long time.

"There have also been several other bonded lifetimes, but this time, Patricia did not want to be alone, mourning Terri. She is going through a difficult time now because of the separation. She knows she left her life too early, that Terri still has years left to live. But she wanted to make sure she didn't suffer the emotional grief again.

"As for the rest of her family, she has had many lifetimes with them also. They are kind and loving to her and she didn't mean to hurt them. She was just saving herself the terrible pain of mourning that she experienced so many times before. She is doing better now. We have taken her, to calm and prepare her on this plane of existence. She will look in now and then on her family. I hope this soothes your mind. You will be together again." **—Pepita**

She Lost Husband and Son

 Dear Tara: Last year, my husband of three years died suddenly of a heart attack. Eight months before that, we had lost our ten-month-old baby boy. I had no chance to say good-bye to them.

My husband and I only dated for six months before we married, but I felt I had known him forever. He was my best friend. I miss him so much.

The only thing that makes all this easier to accept is my feeling that my husband and son are together. Is there anyway you can verify this for me?

I'm also wondering about something else. I feel that my husband knew he was going to die. He had several dreams about our son coming to get him. One of these dreams he had shortly before he died. In it, our son came back for a day to visit. It was understood that it was only for a visit. My husband was so excited and proud of our son that he took him around town to show him off to friends. While they were downtown, my son told my husband that he wanted to show him something, and they began to float up. My husband got scared and hooked his legs on the ledge of a building. Our son told him·it was okay, he would show him some other time. Then our son continued to float up till he was out of sight. That was the end of the dream. Was our son communicating with his father through this dream? If only I knew that they were together, waiting for me, I'd feel much better. If there is anyway to tell them how much I love and miss them still, please do.

A.W.
Fairbanks, AK

In the contact house was Amanda's husband and son. He handed me the baby so he could write. I looked into an angelic face wrapped in a soft blue cloth. The baby had such a sweet face that I started to cry when I thought of his mother's pain at losing him. The husband started to cry too and said he was sorry. He took the notepad and wrote: "I don't know what to say. I saw the baby above me when I had my attack and I couldn't resist following him. I knew something was happening to my body, but I felt no pain as I followed my child.

"We have been together since I died. He was very glad to see me. He was sorry to have left such loving parents, but he knew I was going to die soon and wouldn't be there for him, so he planned to die first so he could guide me to the light. I have spent many

173

lifetimes with this soul, we are completely attuned. I was devastated along with Amanda when the baby died. I miss Amanda very much, but I felt as though I must be with our baby, so I have not missed being on the earth.

"We have had many lives as mother/son, brothers, soldiers, best friends, associates—we are very connected. I am also very connected to Amanda. She was my sister in a previous life and I have loved her for many incarnations. I can see that she has an exciting life upcoming; she will have love and a chance at life again. I hope that I can give her strength when the time comes to choose another. She must remember the potential we had; she can have that again. I will know her again and love her in another life. I wish her well. I will always take care of our baby. My love eternal." **—Your Loving Husband**

Note from Abenda: "Your husband perceives the baby as a baby during this transitional phase. The soul of your baby is in reality as adult as his parents and will soon take a form that is comfortable to him. Amanda, you must fulfill your future destiny and do not be afraid. You have known love, you can find it again. Keep sending love to your husband and child, and remember to love yourself."

Chapter Seven

My Technique

In this chapter, I am going to provide some general background information about spirit guides. Then I'll share how to create your own comfortable area or inner temple to contact your spirit guides. Finally, I'll describe my technique for automatic writing, and give you a sample script to assist you.

Spirit Guides

Spirit guides are loving discarnate entities who assist you to attain spiritual awareness. Every person on the earth has what I call a primary guide, who has been with you since birth and will remain with you throughout your life, always doing everything within their power to assist you in accomplishing your mission on earth. No one is permitted to incarnate upon the earth without a primary guide. Some people call the primary guide a "lifetime" guide; others refer to them as their "guardian angels."

People often wonder if you can have more than one

guide, and the answer is yes. I call these other guides "support guides." Your primary guide will call in these support guides to assist you because they may have expertise or information that is relevant to your situation.

Since there is neither male nor female sex on the other side, your guide will choose an appearance that they feel comfortable with. This usually seems to be the way they looked in their last incarnation, at whatever they considered to be their ideal age.

The guides you have are the guides you deserve. One of the Universal Laws is the Divine Law of Attraction, or "like attracts like." So you get the kind of guides that you have earned in your past lives. Love is the power behind the guidance, and you must realize that it is you who has asked your guide for this inner direction to assist you in remaining on your chosen path of learning. Although your guides are there to protect you, they cannot interfere with your karma. But they will assist you to remain on the path that you chose to walk on this earth to evolve spiritually.

It is a mistake, however, once you establish communication with your spirit guide, to give them too much power. You must always use your own judgment about advice received in these subjective communications. If any unseen voice uses bad language or tells you exactly what to do, immediately cease communication. Evolved souls won't command you—they will gently show you the "light." Your guide never exerts excessive influence; instead he gently points you down the proper path.

Always be aware that you are in control in a meditation. If you feel uncomfortable in any way, just count yourself up from one to five, and say "wide awake." One way to protect yourself is to use a white-light protection technique as part of the session. I'll provide the ritual that both Richard and I use before altered-state-of-consciousness sessions as part of the Automatic Writing Script. The more peaceful and harmonious you are, the easier it will be to directly communicate with your spirit guides.

Creating Your Contact Area
Or Temple Room

Many of you already have your own contact room or temple area, but for those who don't, I'll briefly describe how to create an environment. Once you have relaxed yourself with a few minutes of deep breathing, go into an altered state using the same ascension technique that is described in the next section. You'll always use the ascension technique when doing automatic writing, but you'll only create the temple room once, unless you like to redecorate a lot. Once the room exists in your mind, it will always be available to you.

Okay, you have done a body relaxation, invoked the white light protection ritual, and ascended the stairs (as per the script on page 181). Now you're ready to open the temple room door and step into your room. The room is empty when you first enter; just the walls, floor, ceiling, the door, and a large window. Go to the window and look at the view. Create the environment that you consider the most beautiful in the world. For some, it may be an ocean view. Others will want the mountains, or a forest. Maybe you would prefer the calmness of unbroken, endless fields of wheat, or a panoramic view of your favorite city, from which the temple room offers a private retreat.

Next, turn your attention to the room itself. Because this is going to be your own, private retreat, you want it to feel completely comfortable, a room that is conducive to peaceful meditation. So look around now. What is on the floor? Is it carpeting, or beautifully varnished hardwood floors with Oriental carpets or hand-woven rugs scattered around? Or is it a beautiful tile floor? Next, visualize the furniture. You need to have at least two places to sit, and preferably more. Maybe a large couch or futon, and two or three easy chairs. You can add other furniture as desired—tables, lamps, sculptures, paintings—however you would ideally furnish your private retreat. Maybe you'll want to have a beautiful roll-top desk to work at, or perhaps you'll want to hang pictures of loved ones or people you admire.

As I said in the beginning, Abenda and I created an additional temple room where I could take the concerns and questions of readers for automatic writing responses. I call that contact room my garden house because it is made of glass, like a greenhouse environment. When I look out the window, I see peaceful rolling hills covered with wildflowers. The sunshine has a very intense, white cast to it, so that the garden and my garden room are continually bathed in protective white light. The room is furnished in French Provincial. I have an old English tea trolley near the couch and I frequently serve tea and cake to the different guides who come to answer readers' questions. I also have a yellow legal pad and pens handy for the writers to use, and as they write, my physical hand is moving and writing. Abenda and I decorated this room together, so the room also reflects Abenda's tastes. My own personal temple room is furnished Persian style.

Spend enough time in your temple room to become completely comfortable in the environment. You can use this room for any altered state process, not just automatic writing. Know that this room is your very own, personal retreat from the world where you can come to rest, recharge your spirit, and reaffirm your faith in yourself and your spirituality. It's a place where you find strength, and a place where you seek answers. You can come here at any time and know peace. After you have created this room and are familiar with it, you won't need to repeat the creation process unless you desire to completely change the environment. It's kind of like moving; once you're in, you're in until you leave.

Description of the Automatic Writing Technique

First I'll describe the process, then I'll give you a sample script. Before you start, find a quiet, comfortable place where you won't be disturbed. If necessary, turn off the phone, or turn the ringer down so it doesn't disturb you. I always have one note pad and two pens on my lap, and I know exactly what questions I want to ask in the altered state. I write my questions at the top of the page. You'll begin with your eyes closed, but will open your eyes later when you start to write.

I close my eyes, breathe deeply and start relaxing my body until I feel myself becoming numb and any muscle tension fades away. Next, I use my protection ritual. Then I imagine myself walking down a trail that leads through a forest to a meadow, where I see an ancient stairway with steps of well-worn grey stone. I reach out and touch the stairs, then I start to ascend. I physically feel myself walking up the stairs, higher and higher and higher, until eventually I come to the doorway of my temple. My guide Abenda greets me at the door, and we hug and talk about general affairs before entering the room. We sit on the couch and I ask my questions. If they are about my personal life, Abenda writes. If I am asking about family or friends, I call an entity who guides or loves them. When they appear, I ask them to sit on the couch and hand them the pad of paper and a pen. Visualize handing them the notebook and a pen, and ask that they write legibly about your inquiry.

Now open your eyes sleepily, just enough to see the paper. I like to write in dim light, but once you're used to doing it, you'll be able to write anywhere. I even do automatic writing on airplanes. Stare blankly at the paper without focusing. You want to make sure you're not writing on top of your writing, but don't concentrate upon what is coming through. Just let it happen. You can read it after you count yourself awake at the end of the session.

Not everyone is able to do automatic writing immediately. To break through, the most important suggestion I can give you is to trust yourself and the validity of your thoughts. I also suggest that you keep your hand moving. Just do ovals across the page to keep the energy flowing until something comes through. If after a few minutes your hand doesn't begin to write on its own and a strong thought is coming through, go ahead and write it down. Then return to the ovals. People often break through, by perceiving psychic thoughts they communicate to paper. When the information is verified, they become more trusting and eventually let go and allow themselves to be a channel. If it doesn't work the first time, keep practicing. It can take time to develop new abilities.

When the session is over, I thank the guides who have shared their wisdom with me, and thank my guide Abenda. I may remain in the room after the spirit guides have gone, or we may all leave at the same time. They go back to the astral plane and I awaken to full beta consciousness with a note pad full of the awareness they have shared.

Automatic Writing Script

(The following script is a variation of a seminar session I conduct and have recorded on cassette. You can memorize it and mentally go through the process, or have a friend read it, or record it yourself on cassette. Just speak the words slowly, as if you were very bored. That will be enough to put anyone into trance, including yourself.)

Close your eyes and make yourself perfectly comfortable. Just completely relax. Breathe deeply and relax completely. Breathe through your nose and exhale through your mouth. Ver-r-r-ry deeply, very, ver-r-r-y deeply. And feel calm and peaceful, relaxed and at ease. Calm and peaceful, relaxed and at ease.

(Repeat above two or three times)

181

And now imagine the relaxing power coming into your feet and relaxing your feet. Feel your feet relaxing. Relaxing. And your feet are relaxing. And the relaxing power moves on up your legs, relaxing your lower legs. Relaxing your lower legs. And now on up your legs, relaxing your upper legs. Relaxing your upper legs.

And now feel the relaxing power move on up into your hands, relaxing your hands. And on up into your forearms, relaxing your forearms. And on up into your upper arms, relaxing your upper arms. And your fingers and hands and forearms and upper arms are now just completely relaxed. And the relaxing power now moves on down into the base of your spine, relaxing your spine. And the relaxing power moves slowly up your spine...up your spine...up your spine...and into the back of your neck and shoulder muscles. Relaxing your neck and shoulder muscles. And the relaxing power now moves on up the back of your neck and into your scalp, relaxing your scalp, and draining down into your facial muscles...relaxing your facial muscles.

And your entire body is now relaxed all over in every way. All tension is gone from your body and mind, and you now draw down a bright white light. This is the Universal light of life energy, the God light. Imagine a beam of intense, shimmering light coming down from above and entering your crown chakra of spirituality on the top of your head. Create the light with the unlimited power of your mind. Feel the light begin to flow through your body and mind.

(Ten seconds of silence)

And the light is now concentrating around your heart

area, and you imagine it emerging from your heart area to totally surround your body in a protective aura of white God light.

(Ten seconds of silence)

(White Light Ritual) I call out to the positive powers of the Universe, to my guides and Masters and those who share my energy. I seek Thy protection from all things seen and unseen, all forces and all elements. I open to the light, I offer my body, my mind and my spirit to the light. Let Thy Divine will and mine be as one. I seek to expand the light within and I seek a tranquil mind and harmony with Divine Law. I thank Thee in advance for the enfolding visions, spiritual awareness and healing that awaits me. As above, so below. I ask it, I beseech it, and I mark it, and so it is.

And now imagine yourself outside in the country on a clear summer night. The sky is full of stars and it feels good to be here. You feel safe and secure as you look up at the blanket of stars. You hear the sounds of the night. *(Pause)* Imagine this very, very vividly. Be there.

(One minute)

It feels so good to be here, looking up at the stars and enjoying the night. And it's now time to draw down the Universal energy of the stars, so please imagine yourself drawing down the light—drawing down the energy of the stars—the positive powers of the universe. *(Pause)* Perceive this energy as being drawn down into the form of an illumination that enters your crown chakra on the top of your head. *(Pause)* So do this now. Actually draw down the energy, and allow it to become your reality.

(Alternate White Light Ritual or use both) The Universal energy of the stars...Draw down the light...the positive powers of the Universe...the God light...the star light...the love light...let it happen...let it be...drawing down the Universal energy of the stars...the light of the Universe....

(One minute)

And you are now filled with light and you look to the eastern horizon to see the sky becoming lighter and lighter and lighter. *(Pause)* And as the sun rises, you offer thanks for all you have and all that you may become.

(Thirty seconds)

And the Sun is now above the horizon and it feels warm on your skin...and you notice a trail off to your left. It's time to follow this trail. It leads off into the trees...into the trees...and you sense the coolness in the shadows, and you inhale the rich scent of the earth and foliage as you walk the path. The early-morning dew is still damp on the grass and sunlight flickers through the rustling tree leaves. And as you walk the path, you hear birds and subtle sounds of the awakening forest.

(Thirty seconds)

And ahead of you, the path becomes brighter as it widens and ends at a beautiful meadow...and right in the middle of the meadow are stairs ascending up into the sky. Take a moment to perceive the meadow and stairs.

(Five seconds)

Go ahead, walk into the meadow where the gentle breeze rustles the grass and tosses your hair. Butterflies flutter around you but your attention is focused upon the stairs...stairs that ascend into the clouds...stairs that shimmer like polished marble...ascending...familiar stairs ascending up into the heavens. You walk over to the stairs and touch them.

(Five seconds)

You know the stairs lead up to your sacred temple, and you want to ascend them. Follow your inner direction and begin to ascend the stairs. Go ahead...go ahead...climb the stairs. It's safe to climb the stairs, so go ahead and climb higher and higher and higher. See and feel yourself climbing higher and higher and higher.

(Five seconds)

Climbing higher and higher and higher.

(Five seconds)

And you're climbing higher and higher and higher— until you eventually come to the doorway of your sacred temple.

(Five seconds)

And the doorway is now there before you. See it. *(Pause)* Feel it. *(Pause)* Go ahead and open the door, go inside, and perceive your sacred temple. Visualize the architecture and decor very, very vividly. Notice that on the other side of the room, there is an arched opening that leads out onto the astral planes.

(Twenty seconds)

This is your special place to come to feel better...to recharge and reaffirm your faith in yourself and your spirituality. It's a place to find strength, a place to seek answers. Even weeks from now, months from now, years from now, you can come here and know peace. So take some time to arrange your temple to your liking. Maybe you want to make some changes or add some

furnishings. Your imagination will result in manifesta-
tion…Go ahead, be creative.

*(Pause for as long as you need to create the temple
room in your first session)*

And now, your spirit guide is entering the room
through the archway to the astral planes. Go ahead and
welcome your guide. You can communicate with
thought language by simply asking a question with a
thought, and listening as your guide answers you with a
returning thought.

(Thirty seconds)

Your guide will protect you from all things seen and
unseen, all forces and all elements. And you are relaxed
and at ease, and it is time to sit down and perceive
answers through automatic writing. Take a moment to
meditate upon who you would like to write through your
hand and what you want to ask.

(Thirty seconds)

All right, it's now time for you and your guide to call
in the entity you want to communicate awareness. So go
ahead and call out to them. Hear your mental voice
echoing out across the universe as you draw the entity
to you.

(Fifteen seconds)

And the entity you have called is now entering through
the archway from the astral plane. Ask them to come and
sit next to you. Perceive this vividly. *(Pause)* And now,
hand them a notebook and a pen, and ask that they write
legibly about your inquiry. *(Pause)* And as they write,
you take a deep breath and let the writing come through
your earthly presence. You now begin to write with your

hand. You can simply transfer your thoughts from your mind to the paper until such time as the pen takes off all on its own. So go ahead, let the writing flow. Trust yourself. You are a channel for the light and awareness flows through you now.

(Leave at least fifteen minutes to write)

All right, it is time to end this session and to thank the entity for sharing. So go ahead.

(Five seconds)

And it is now time to return, so thank your guide and say good-bye.

(Five seconds)

And you now leave your sacred temple room, knowing you can return at any time you desire to do so. And you begin to descend the stairs...descending, descending, descending...coming back now *(pause)* remembering everything you experienced in this peaceful meditation. *(Pause)* And on the count of five, you will awaken filled with joy, at peace with yourself, the world and everyone in it. Number one, coming on up and remembering everything. Sense an expanding spiritual light within. Number two, coming on up, at peace with all life and remembering everything. Number three, coming up, feeling balance and harmony. Number four, coming on up, recalling the situation and the room. And number five, wide awake, wide awake. Open your eyes and feel good. Number five, wide awake.

* * * * *

For those who prefer to work with a prerecorded tape, I have created a beautiful guided meditation called "Automatic Writing" (Item TS205—$9.98), which uses a variation of this script and is available through **Valley of the Sun**. Side B contains the same beautiful music as on side A, but without my verbalization. Use it on your own, after you have become familiar with the technique and no longer need to be guided.

The more you develop this technique, the more effective it will become. Everyone has the power and ability to become proficient at automatic writing. With dedication and practice, you can expect the same results I obtain in my temple room.

Good luck with your own automatic writing. Go in peace and do your best.

About The Author

Tara Sutphen describes herself as an "occultist." In addition to her automatic writing specialty, she is a master-level palmist and often publicly demonstrates her abilities at handwriting analysis, personology, somatotyping and astrology, combined with psychic ability, to accurately read people.

Tara has often used her automatic writing to assist her husband Dick Sutphen in his research, as is evidenced in his book **Earthly Purpose** (Pocket Books). Tara's column, "Cause & Effect," is a regular feature in *Master of Life WINNERS* magazine. Together, the Sutphens annually conduct their popular seminars in at least a dozen cities throughout the country. They live in Malibu, California, with their three children, two horses, three cats and three dogs.

FREE SUBSCRIPTION
(Just Send Us Your Receipt For This Book)

Master of Life WINNERS is a quarterly magazine sent FREE to all Valley of the Sun book/ tape buyers and seminar attendees. We'll be glad to mail you a free sample issue, or if you'll send us your receipt for this book, we'll send the magazine free for a year.

Each issue is approximately 100 pages and contains news, research reports and articles on the subjects of metaphysics, psychic exploration and self-help, in addition to information on all Sutphen Seminars, and over 350 audio and video tapes: hypnosis, meditation, sleep programming, subliminal programming, silent subliminals, and New Age music. A sampling of some of our audio and video tapes and books that relate to the content of **Blame It On Your Past Lives** will be found on the following pages.

Valley of the Sun Publishing
Box 3004, Agoura Hills, CA 91376
Phone: 818/889-1575

Audio Tapes That Relate To This Book
Available Through Your Local Metaphysical Bookseller
Or Directly From Valley of the Sun Publishing

AUTOMATIC WRITING
By Tara Sutphen
A Beautiful Guided Meditation
To Explore The Powerful Process
Of Automatic Writing

Side A: Now you can experience this powerful process on your own. Tara duplicates her own stairway to the astral plane and guides you through the ascension process. At the top of the stairs is your "sacred temple room." At the back of the room is an open archway leading out onto the astral plane. It is from here that your contacts will enter. Your spirit guide is called in, and the technique is clearly explained before you begin automatic writing. **Side B:** The same beautiful music used on side A.s In time, you'll use it to ascend all on your own. One hour, one cassette, packaged in a book-size slipcase.

.... TS205—$9.98

SHAMAN JOURNEY
By Tara Sutphen
A Beautiful Guided Meditation
To Explore Your Joys, Burdens,
Goals & New Directions

Side A: Tara gently induces an altered state of consciousness. You are then directed to a peaceful mountain meadow where an Indian Shaman awaits you. The Indian will guide you to his tepee where you experience rituals of brotherhood before your journey starts. On horseback you set off in the four directions in search of personal awareness. You'll become one with an eagle, a deer and a bear as you discover life-changing insights and special messages from Higher Mind. **Side B:** Thirty minutes of the beautiful clay flute music from Side A. One hour, one cassette, packaged in a book-size slipcase.

.... TS202—$9.98

VISION QUEST
By Tara Sutphen
A Beautiful Guided Meditation
To Explore Psychic Solutions
& Visit Your Sacred Place

Side A: Tara gently induces an altered state of consciousness. Your quest begins in a Sedona-like environment and proceeds through several uplifting explorations until you begin to ask psychic questions. In the altered state, you can expect to receive awareness-expanding answers from Higher Mind. After this, you will continue to your sacred place, an environment you will create to your liking, to find peace and higher understanding." **Side B:** Thirty minutes of the beautiful clay flute music from Side A. One hour, one cassette, packaged in a book-size slipcase.

.... TS201—$9.98

WALK OF LIFE
By Tara Sutphen
A Beautiful Guided Meditation
To Explore The Unrecognized Forces
At Play In Your Life

Side A: Tara induces an altered state of consciousness. You are then guided through a forested area to a clearing bordering a river, where you are drawn to an altar with a special gift for your journey. You'll take a small boat down the river through your fears. Each step of the process helps you to better understand yourself and to allow subconscious awareness to surface, so that you may better deal with the forces that influence, motivate and restrict your life. **Side B:** Thirty minutes of the beautiful music from Side A. One hour, one cassette, packaged in a book-size slipcase.

.... TS204—$9.98

Other Titles That Relate To This Book
Available Through Your Local Metaphysical Bookseller
Or Directly From Valley of the Sun Publishing

PAST-LIFE REGRESSION
RX17® Audio Tape

Contains a metaphysical induction that is ultra-powerful and totally enjoyable.

Side One contains a basic introductory session in which you'll experience one of your past lifetimes. Once you are proficient with Side One, move on to the more advanced session on Side Two, which is a past-life regression that you direct. You decide what you want to explore; you can choose a different life each time you listen.

.... RX201—$12.50

PAST-LIFE REGRESSION
Video Hypnosis®

Contains visual and verbal hypnosis, audio and video subliminals.

Examples of Suggestions: You can now perceive your past lives. ■ You can trust your thoughts and fantasies. ■ Past-life awareness can release you. ■ Let the past-life impressions flow into your mind. ■ You have the ability to receive vivid impressions of your past lives. ■ You now let past-life impressions flow into your mind.

.... VHS129—$19.95

SPIRIT GUIDES
2-Tape Audio Album

Make contact with your spirit guides—loving entities that are drawn to you to help you attain spiritual awareness.

Tapes 1A & 1B: Your Spirit Guides—A one-hour discussion of your guides.

Tape 2A: Spirit Guides Workshop—A guided meditation/hypnosis session.

Tape 2B: Meditation/Altered-State Session—A contact meditation follows the chakra balancing induction.

Includes two tapes and a 96-page instruction manual.

.... C857—$24.95

THE SOULMATE PROCESS
By Bob Lancer

The Soulmate Process is a practical book on releasing blocks and directing energy to manifest a soulmate relationship (or transform an existing relationship). You **can** have the wonderful, magical, miraculous relationship you long for.

It not only explains what you can do to obtain the love of your life, it also guides you through exercises and procedures that engage you as an active participant, actually *doing* things to help yourself. Several stories illustrate the journeys, challenges and triumphs others experienced as they used **The Soulmate Process** in their quest for love.

Beautiful full-color cover, printed on acid-free paper. 128 page trade-size paperback.
.... B928—$9.98

REINVENTING YOURSELF
By Dick Sutphen

Reinventing Yourself is a complete metaphysical self-renewal system. Dick has formulized and added to the trainer techniques he has used so effectively for 15 years in human-potential seminars. Now, with simplified explanations and dialog examples, he provides a unique and extremely powerful system to find your own blocks. Next, you explore the action required to eliminate the problem, followed by the encouragement to create a new reality.

Reinventing Yourself is for those whose life isn't bad, but it just isn't good, as well as for people with real problems.

Beautiful full-color cover, printed on acid-free paper. 180 page trade-size paperback.
.... B927—$9.98

Other Titles That Relate To This Book

Available Through Your Local Metaphysical Bookseller
Or Directly From Valley of the Sun Publishing

THE SPIRITUAL PATH GUIDEBOOK
By Dick Sutphen

For twenty years, Sutphen has taught metaphysics, conducted seminars and written some of the all-time bestselling books on the subject. In **The Spiritual Path Guidebook**, he condenses this wisdom down to hundreds of short, life-changing concepts and presents them in this easy-to-assimilate format. 128 page meditation-size paperback with a beautiful full-color cover, printed on acid-free paper.
.... B927—$5.95

HEART MAGIC
By Dick Sutphen

Mystical stories about finding love and answers by one of the world's bestselling New Age authors.

The incredible stories include: **Soulmate Location Service, The Other Lindy, Beneath Sedona, Auric Light, The Walk-In; Those Who Share Our Energy; Guardian Angel; Greater Good; The Chair,** and **The Beginning.**

Beautiful full-color cover, printed on acid-free paper. 256 page trade-size paperback.
.... B926—$9.98
